HORRORSCOPES

Exorcise the monsters within and unleash
the scary side of your sun sign

Stella Hyde
author of *Darkside Zodiac*

WEISER BOOKS
San Francisco, CA / Newburyport, MA

First published in 2014 by Weiser Books
Red Wheel/Weiser, LLC
With offices at:
665 Third Street, Suite 400
San Francisco, CA 94107
www.redwheelweiser.com

Library of Congress Cataloging-in-Publication Data
available upon request

This book was conceived, designed, and produced
by Paperwasp, an imprint of Balley Design Limited,
The Loft, 45 Grantham Road,
Brighton, East Sussex, BN1 6EF, UK
www.paperwaspbooks.com

creative director: Dr. Lucian Starr (*demon firestarter*)
designer: Mathilda Mitchell (*demon king*)
text: Stella Hyde (*weremom*)
project editor: Tabitha Bell (*count dracula*)
illustrations: Mathilda Mitchell (*demon king*)

ISBN: 978-1-57863-569-6

Printed in China
10 9 8 7 6 5 4 3 2 1

CONTENTS

We've all got monsters within, otherwise we would all behave better, and the world would be a wonderful place, but to call them all demons is just lazy. What is that ravening beast that bursts from your guts and savages whatever it sees when you are, say, crossed in love, overlooked for a promotion, held up in line, disrespected, or are just feeling mean, ornery, or bored? You could spend months of precious time and truckloads of cash in therapy wrestling with the horror within, but before you do that, why not take a look at your sun sign?

Before we get going, don't expect a named monster. As all astro fans know, sun sign astrology is kind of broadscale; Rams, for example, are all born between March 21 and April 20, but to hone things down to the individual lovable Aries that is you in particular, all sorts of variables come into play to add refinements and rococo flourishes: rising signs, moon placement, planetary aspects and angles, conjunctions, oppositions, sextiles, trines, nodes—getting a bit astrotecchie here, so you will just have to take my word for it; and it's the same on the monstrous Darkside. So, no, I cannot ID your personal monster as Zuul, the Kraken, Nosferatu, insert-monster-of-choice here, or specify which of the *Twilight* crew you are: but I can tell you which one of the four major monster tribes you belong to: Demon, Vampire, Ghost, or Werewolf. It's all to do with Elements and Energies, and you can read all about it on pages 8–9.

So, what are you going to do when you have identified your monster? Well that's up to you, but I have to point out that neither I, nor the publishers, nor anyone who has had anything to do with the book can be held responsible in any way.

How this book works

Each sun sign is covered in zodiacal order. (I trust you know your sun sign otherwise you wouldn't be here, but the dates are given in case you are having a blank moment.) Each section starts with a rundown of your normal self, the Dr. Jekyll you, then moves swiftly onto the Mr. Hyde persona you think no one else knows about. Mr. Hyde is the part of you that lets the wrong ones in…he is the portal for your monster.

The elements and energy associated with your sun sign give us the tribe your monster belongs to, and you'll find out (although you probably already know) how it manifests, what it does, and whether, when confronted, you own up to it, feel ashamed of it, are in denial, secretly adore it, or use it to your best advantage.

Then it's time for a little finesse, finding out how the zodiacal variables, such as your rising sign and Moon placement modify your monster and what your ruling planet's got to do with it.

And now, and this is the best bit, we look at how your monster behaves in the real world—what triggers it, what happens when it is in love, what happens when it's at work, and what, if anything, you can do to tame it. And finally, in compliance with Safety and Health Regulations there is some advice for the rest of us about how we can defend ourselves.

And a final tip: don't just read your sun sign. If you know your rising sign, and where your Moon is, read the sections that cover those signs as well, to get a fuller monster experience.

* To find out where your Moon is placed, what your rising sign is, and other variables, you can get yourself a free birthchart online. For best results you should know the date, place, and time (within two hours of your birth). There are many fine sites; try: www.cafeastrology.com or https://alabe.com

The Monster Element

Monsters were forged in another time in a different dimension, before logic and rationality ruined the world, and are a fusion of the four basic elements (Fire, Earth, Air, and Water); there is, of course, a fifth element and that is the energy that animates them. So if you want to know what kind of monster your sun sign has stuck you with, you must look at the element that rules your sign and the energy (aka quality or mode, in astro talk) that drives it. The three energies are: cardinal, the source, raw energy; fixed, contained and consolidated energy; and mutable, scattered and atomized energy.

The zodiac is cleverly, mystically even, constructed around two interweaving sequences. The four elements appear in this order; Fire, Earth, Air, Water; and the three energies run like this: Cardinal, Fixed, and Mutable. This means that each element has three signs and each energy has four. So when you run the sequence together every sign has a unique combination of element and energy.

Each of the elements spawns a different kind of monster, and each monster is horrific in a slightly different way, depending on the energy. Look in the panels to find what kind if monster you are hosting.

Fire and Demons

Fire is the first element: big, obvious, and proud of it. It's the flickering face of both creativity and destruction. Hell is more or less entirely made from Fire so unsurprisingly Fire spawns the tribe of Demons, who are most at home in the infernal regions. What class of Demon you are depends on your sign's energy. For a detailed portrait, check out your sun sign entry.

Zodiacal Demons are

Aries—Cardinal sign • *Leo—Fixed sign* • *Sagittarius—Mutable sign*

Earth and Vampires

Earth is the second element, the useful, permanent one. It's all about growth and guardianship, but it needs to combine with fire or water to create. Earth spawns Vampires, who are immortal, yet need the energy of others to flourish and only feel safe surrounded by their element. What class of Vampire you are depends on your sign's energy. For a more detailed portrait, check out your sun sign entry.

Zodiacal Vampires are

Capricorn—Cardinal sign • *Taurus—Fixed sign* • *Virgo—Mutable sign*

Air and Ghosts

Air is the third element, the one we can't see but can feel. Free and unconfined, it has no fixed abode and laughs at barriers. Air is invisible, gets everywhere, and can change temperature and density at will, so it is the element that spawns Ghosts. What class of Ghost you are depends on your sign's energy. For a more detailed portrait, check out your sun sign entry.

Zodiacal Ghosts are

Libra—Cardinal sign • *Aquarius—Fixed sign* • *Gemini—Mutable sign*

Water and Werewolves

Water is the fourth element. It's the one that we are mostly made of, at once incredibly powerful yet under the sway of the Moon, which can pull it out of shape on a regular basis, so it is the element that spawns Werewolves. What class of Werewolf you are depends on your sign's energy. For a more detailed portrait, check out your sun sign entry.

Zodiacal Werewolves are

Cancer—Cardinal sign • *Scorpio—Fixed sign* • *Pisces—Mutable sign*

ARIES

Aries the Ram • March 21–April 20 • Cardinal Fire Sign
 • Positive Sign • Ruled by: Mars

You Jekyll...

On the outside you are a mild-mannered Ram with friends and family, a normal life, a job, blameless hobbies, a few endearingly annoying little ways, but basically one of nature's white sheep. Well, to be accurate, as an Aries you aren't all that mild-mannered, and long-suffering friends and family may have something to say about your little ways, but wotthehell, you get stuff done.

Aries is the leader of the zodiac pack, the first sign—raw, unsocialized, invigorating, unstoppable ego, never at home to the Lord of Despair. Ruled by the element of Fire, and the planet Mars, you are, at your best, the stuff from which heroes are hewn.

...you Hyde

Everybody knows how heroes can flip to the dark side in an instant, and become their own evil twin. Look what happened when Superman went bad. In your case, Aries, what happens is that your focused energy plus an awesome lack of self-doubt, a pathological drive to be in charge, and a very short fuse come together and propel you from hero to despot in one superbound. You are the zodiac's two-year old, and on a bad day, its sadistic bully (albeit a rather predictable one because sophistication isn't your thing).

Your accessory of choice is a chainsaw even if you aren't from Texas. The blood and guts you spill are not always your own.

Aries: the Demon Firestarter

You are a Cardinal Fire sign. Of all the zodiacal elemental/energy combos, this is the no-brainer. Cardinal signs lead, which in a good way is a great relief to the rest of us, but on the monstrous side means heading straight for the hellmouth and taking the rest of us with them. Familiar? Cardinal signs are the quintessence of their element. In Aries' case, this is fire, uncomplicated stuff that is either on or off, good or bad, and can toggle from either state in a nanosecond.

So it's no surprise that the Aries monster of choice is the Demon, the spawn of hellfire. (Although, of course, you would not accept it was choice, as that would imply some sort of responsibility.) A straightforward fallen (or pushed) angel who meant well at the time, but somehow it all went wrong, although you have forgotten how, because you don't do detail. Demons come in all shapes and sizes, and as an enthusiastic multitasker with a very short attention span, you have probably channeled every one of them. Sometimes, it's enough just to be adorably impish, and other times you can come on as the Lord of the Pit, with extra stench. As long as fire is involved, actually or metaphorically, you aren't fussy.

Far from feeling shame, remorse, existential despair, or railing against the Supreme Being, Manifest Destiny, or your heartbreaking trailer park childhood for your behavior, you just don't notice. Introspection is not your strong suit. Neither would you claim to have been possessed and therefore unblameable for your demonic excess. You do what you do— scraping out eyeballs with a spoon, hurling victims into the pit of ordure, turning people inside out, etc.—but, you shrug, that's what Demons do.

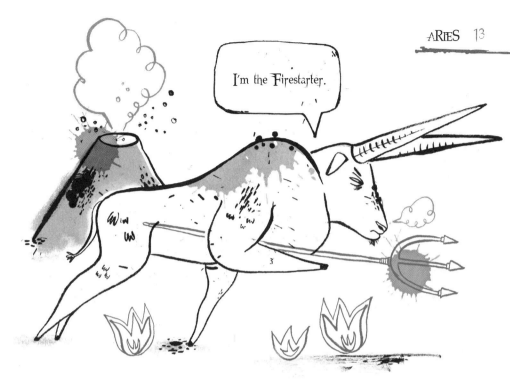

So how do you manifest?

You usually look just like yourself, only bigger and redder, although it sometimes feels as if you've grown an extra head. (You have more than enough energy to effect spectacular transformations if you wanted to—black scales, breath of fire, etc.—but it seems unnecessary finessing as far as you are concerned.) Demons are normally summoned, but any Aries worth his or her pitchfork won't wait around for all that black candles and badly drawn runes tedium; plus you don't appreciate being at anyone's beck and call. You go when you want to. As your demon dial is superglued to 11, and you aren't that good at judging the moment (your moment is the perpetual NOW!) you often fail to match the demonic manifestation with the circumstances, get it wrong and devastate a couple of continents over who moved your cheese, but go no further than a fiendish cackle when you get your pink slip. However, as you aren't the Demon of Consistency, no one can ever tell when and how you are going to spring from your pit to terrorize us. You like it like that.

[For other demons in the zodiac see Leo and Sagittarius]

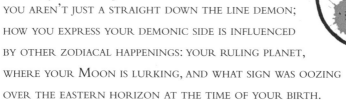

Other Evil Influences

YOU AREN'T JUST A STRAIGHT DOWN THE LINE DEMON;
HOW YOU EXPRESS YOUR DEMONIC SIDE IS INFLUENCED
BY OTHER ZODIACAL HAPPENINGS: YOUR RULING PLANET,
WHERE YOUR MOON IS LURKING, AND WHAT SIGN WAS OOZING
OVER THE EASTERN HORIZON AT THE TIME OF YOUR BIRTH.

Bad moon

Your Moon expresses the Inner You. In your case, Aries, there isn't much of an Inner
You. Bigger monsters trying to turn you inside out are in for a disappointment.
Demons may come from another dimension, but they don't have many themselves.
Your Moon can be placed in any of the zodiac houses when you are born and
modify your monster (although not in a good way, of course). Here's how it affects
the Aries Demon:

MOON IN ARIES *The demon's Demon;*
unadulterated full-fat "demontude."
MOON IN TAURUS *A greedy vampiric*
Demon; sucks blood, makes sausages out of it.
MOON IN GEMINI *Naughty shapeshifting*
Demon, light on its claws, can disappear at will.
MOON IN CANCER *Passive-aggressive*
Demon—always late when summoned, but
always brings hot cakes.
MOON IN LEO *Spectacular Demon with extra*
flame-throwing capacity and an agent to deal
with all that tedious summoning business.
MOON IN VIRGO *The Demon that has*
turned nagging into Geneva-convention busting
torture, but who cleans up after itself.

MOON IN LIBRA *Indolent Demon, will only*
get out of bed to terrify A-list
MOON IN SCORPIO *Incubus. Or Succubus.*
MOON IN SAGITTARIUS *Clumsy and*
tactless Demon, always knocking over black
altars and scuffing out pentacles by mistake.
MOON IN CAPRICORN *The Demon that*
invoices for its services and will only work with
CEOs of financial institutions.
MOON IN AQUARIUS *Groovy Demon with a*
great line in snappy one-liners; once appeared in
Buffy the Vampire Slayer *and has never really*
got over it.
MOON IN PISCES *The Demon name-checked*
in the demon drink.

How does your planet bring out your demon?

It fuels your demonic fury, generating an unending supply of raw rage. Aries is ruled by Mars—planet thug. It glowers in the night sky, like an angry red eyeball in the socket of an obsidian skull (poetic, eh?). Named for the Roman god of war and destruction (Aries likes the obvious) it even has two demonic moons called Phobos and Deimos, aka fear and loathing. And it's hot: a demon's home away from home.

What's that coming over the hill?

The sign rising over the eastern horizon when you were spawned represents your public persona; in this case, this means what kind of Demon you might look like when possessed, or how you would secretly like to manifest in the real world if only you could.

ARIES RISING *Flaming hair, flaming eyes, flaming lips…a Fire Demon with extra propellant.*

TAURUS RISING *Hewn from solid well-barbecued beef, thick neck, blood-red eyes; I'm thinking minotaur.*

GEMINI RISING *A flickering two-headed Demon with eight limbs, two pairs of crimson-tinted shades, and forked but silvery tongues.*

CANCER RISING *Demon almost entirely fireproofed by heavy armor plating made of chiton and mom's bad-apple pie; scarlet beads for eyes.*

LEO RISING *Enormous, devilishly hot Demon with a hide of emeralds, eyes of molten red gold, and diamonds on the soles of its hooves.*

VIRGO RISING *Pink-eyed Demon with the thermostat on low; leaves nothing but an over-organized sock drawer and a trail of Clorox when it dematerializes.*

LIBRA RISING *Smoldering elegant Demon, made from mirrored bronze, with ruby eyes and a flamethrower in a Gucci case.*

SCORPIO RISING *All-black demon made of flint and consumed by its own heat, with nothing at all where the red eyes usually are.*

SAGITTARIUS RISING *Flaming nightmare of a Demon, covered in self-inflicted scorchmarks; rolling red eyes, and heavy on the teeth.*

CAPRICORN RISING *Proper old-school traditional Fire Demon: red eyes, horns, tail, cloven hooves, toasting fork.*

AQUARIUS RISING *Cyberdemon, incandescent with an LED flame-display and infrared visual scanning devices.*

PISCES RISING *Damp, steamy Demon, with smoke damage and a slight stench of kerosene; bloodshot eyes; oozes a lot.*

Living with your monster

LIVING WITH YOUR MONSTER IS A DAILY CHALLENGE IN EVERY SCENARIO. HERE ARE THE ANSWERS TO SOME ARIES FAQS.

What triggers your monster?

It's hard to say with Aries, but anything can set you off: too much detail, paperwork, instructions, not being allowed to do exactly what you want, idiots not doing what you tell them…what traditionally happens is that you roar, lay waste with words, curses, threats, fists, whatever weapon is on hand (fire and the sword if they are available), and in the very worst case, a tank. It's a very short rage, and you rarely remember it, but the rest of us have the afterburn to prove it.

How does your demon do in love?

Sometimes passionate rage can be attractive and flattering. Why do you think the demon lover is such a literary trope, huh? But full-on, all-day Heathcliff can be very wearing for all concerned. As you are always in love, often for several hours at a time, demonic rage may be engendered by the beloved object (a) ignoring you, (b) nagging you (that is, they have an opinion not your own), (c) having a headache, (d) not buying you a gift, (e) buying you gift but not what you wanted, (f) wanting a quiet night in. If you are an Aries male, women want to reform you and exorcise your demon; if you are an Aries female, men want to tame you. You'll have none of that; your demon remains free, you just change partners.

What does your demon do at work?

You did not put Extreme Volatility on your resume, but it's your core strength. Anything can trigger the workday demon; just being at work, for a start: having to do the same thing that you did yesterday, again; being told what to do; instructions; a critique of your Mission Statement (Kill!). Even

Aries has to eat, so unless you are happily employed as a lion tamer, oil rigger, red arrow pilot, fire fighter, horror movie background artiste, hedge fund maverick, etc. and paid to have demonic periods, you have to channel it through cubicle wars, office Olympics, ritual defenestration of office hardware, and the occasional melt down in the stationery cupboard.

How do you tame your monster?

As you don't think your behavior is in any way outré, it takes a time to work out why you would want to. After all, you are simply being justifiably outraged—it's all over (sometimes literally) in seconds; it seems hardly worth bothering. But if circumstances mean you really, really have to curb your inner demon, physical expression is the way forward. Find something inanimate to bash (maybe invest in an anvil?). If you're in the office, wind down with a session or two on Assassin's Creed, even if it's in the middle of the Annual General Meeting (AGM). At the very least carry a pillow or a towel to scream into: I know you don't see why you should, but it's a condition of your Restraining Order.

GETTING PROTECTION

What can the rest of us do to shield ourselves from the fallout? Traditionally, Demons are repelled by salt, holy water, and iron, or contained in a pentacle. I am not sure the iron works with you, as Aries loves hot metal far too much. Holy water is not always on hand. So I would go for the salt. It might not always be practical to throw salt at you (especially as you love a food fight) so maybe we go the more figurative route and simply take everything you do and say with a pinch or six of salt, and pretend that it didn't happen. While you're in full rage mode, the rest of us can draw a quick pentacle—not to contain you, but to stand in ourselves until it's all over.

TAURUS

Taurus the Bull • April 21–May 21 • Fixed Earth Sign
• Negative Sign • Ruled by: Venus

You Jekyll...

The world looks at you and sees a handsome charmer: hardworking, sleek, successful, a calm connoisseur of life's finer things (art, wine, food, chocolate, money, real estate), a teensy bit fixed in your ways, maybe, and perhaps a tad thick around the neck, but an asset to family and society. They call you down to earth; you are flattered.

Taurus is the second sign of the zodiac (you like to plow a ready-made furrow), the reliable henchperson, ruled by the sensible element, Earth, and Venus, the planet of harmony. At your most serene and gracious, you are a fixed, dependable feature in the chaotic landscape of other peoples' lives, unafflicted by self-doubt or too vivid an imagination, a rock in the zodiac's troubled sea.

...you Hyde

The trouble with a rock is that it stands opposite a hard place, handily positioned to grind the rest of us into chopped liver. A lifetime of being The Reliable One convinces you that the only way to do anything is your way. Anyone who deviates from Right Thinking risks confrontation with half a ton of angry pot-roast. Your appreciation of fine things segues seamlessly into an obsession with the possession of them—people, stuff, countries…you move slowly, Taurus, but the path from endearing, restful certainty to implacable intransigence is a short one and anyone standing in the way, even if they twirl a red cape, and everything gets trampled into the mud.

Taurus: Count Dracula

You are a Fixed Earth sign. Earth is the element that changes so slowly that to those of us with mayfly-grade attention spans, it appears to stay exactly the same. It may seem that Earth is already as fixed as you can get, and yet you, Taurus, somehow make it feel even fixed-er. Fixed signs do what they say on the label (very Fixed sign of them) and skewer their elements, establishing strongholds, building barriers, marking boundaries, keeping to the Way. On the sunny side of the street, this is a Good Thing: who doesn't love a structure to rail against/pull down? On the monstrous side it sees us covered in dust, trapped for eternity in the ruined castle/doorless dungeon/cold, cold crypt.

Earth. Enclosed space. Implacable desire. A fixation on white throats. (Taurus rules the throat.) Taurus does not do unexpected, so what else could your monster be but a vampire? As you are traditional and like to follow set precedents, not an amber-eyed lightweight of the *Twilight* kind, you model yourself on Bram Stoker's Count: a class act with his own castle who spends half his life in a bespoke Earth-packed coffin. A monster of regular habits (the villagers knew when to hide their buxom daughters and put out a tourist instead); focused on regular meals. He wears a cape, and you bulls know about the Thing with the Cape.

Do you try to hide your vampire? Live a double life? Of course not; that would mean duplicity, which requires imagination. Anyway, you reason, what's so bad about vampires? Strong, tenacious, powerful, sexy, with an ability to lay their fangs on the important things: food, property, wealth. And routine? If it's dark, you're the bat; in the daylight you're the bull.

So how do you manifest?

Very slowly, but inexorably. The room goes quiet as the light and air is slowly sucked out of it; well, that's what it feels like to the rest of us. The veins on your neck knot and throb as you stand very still, generating a beefy forcefield. Even though you don't actually get any bigger, the seams on your Armani suit start straining and popping as you slowly bulk up. Your forehead glows red in the spots where there would be horns. Snorting may occur. Your pupils iris into pinpricks as you focus on the object of your rage. Traditionally vampires can fly—you have never managed that (aerodynamics are against you on this one) but the pawing of the ground indicates a relic-brain attempt at take off. There may be rampaging as your outer bull wrestles with your inner bat. (Real vampire bats feed on cattle; you can't tell me that there hasn't been some kind of morphic crossover somewhere down the line.) And just when it seems you have calmed down, you come back from the dead and gore your tormentors in the neck, probably metaphorically.

[For other vampires in the zodiac see Virgo and Capricorn]

Other Evil Influences

HOWEVER HARD YOU WORK AT IT, YOU ARE NOT
SIMPLY A STOKER CLONE; HOW YOU EXPRESS YOUR VAMPIRE STYLE IS
INFLUENCED BY OTHER ZODIACAL HAPPENINGS: YOUR RULING PLANET,
WHERE YOUR MOON IS LURKING, AND WHAT SIGN WAS OOZING OVER
THE EASTERN HORIZON AT THE TIME OF YOUR BIRTH.

Bad moon

Your Moon expresses the Inner You. You love a boundary Taurus, and keep your Inner You firmly penned in a separate field so you can't see what it's up to. Your lawyers tell you this is called plausible deniability. Your Moon can be placed in any of the zodiac houses when you are born and modify your monster (although not in a good way, of course). Here's how it affects the Taurus Vampire.

MOON IN ARIES *Enthusiastic, hot-eyed Vampire, likes to make victims' blood boil before drinking.*

MOON IN TAURUS *Gourmet Vampire, goes for organically reared peasants and extra virgin virgins.*

MOON IN GEMINI *Easily bored Vampire, drinks, discards, and sells suck-and-tell tales to the tabloids.*

MOON IN CANCER *Stay-at-home Vampire, much prefers to feed quietly off family and close friends.*

MOON IN LEO *Stylish Vampire, a sucker for blue-blooded victims or red carpet royalty.*

MOON IN VIRGO *Immaculate Vampire, carries pocket vacuum cleaner in case of unexpected disintegration into dust motes.*

MOON IN LIBRA *Indolent Vampire, will not get out the fangs for less than a small chateau in the South of France.*

MOON IN SCORPIO *Vampish Vampire; cannot resist leaden pickup lines before going for the throat.*

MOON IN SAGITTARIUS *Energetic Vampire with extra long fangs, likes to run with the Children of the Night after fueling.*

MOON IN CAPRICORN *Traditional Vampire, tuxedo, cape, fangs, and goat's hooves.*

MOON IN AQUARIUS *Space Vampire, you don't like to hear your victims scream.*

MOON IN PISCES *Unobservant Vampire, you thought you were drinking claret from an unusual throat-shaped cup.*

How does your planet bring out your vampire?

It makes sure that you stay insatiable. Taurus is ruled by Venus, the planetary avatar of a Woman of Appetite who knows what she wants and will stop at nothing to get it, consume it, then get more of it. Draped in creamy clouds, it drifts tantalizingly slowly around the Sun, but underneath it is a raging ball of unquenchable heat. It's named for the Roman goddess of love and harmony, and you know how scary the power of love can be.

What's that coming over the hill?

The sign rising over the eastern horizon when you were made represents your public persona, your outer appearance; in this case, what kind of Vampire you might look like when possessed, or how you would secretly like to manifest in the real world if you could.

ARIES RISING *Mad, red-eyed Vampire, rakishly handsome, Christopher Lee hammering it home.*

TAURUS RISING *A bison in a tuxedo. A buffalo at the ball.*

GEMINI RISING *Twin Vampires, double the seduction rate, just like Brad Pitt and Tom Cruise in* Interview with a Vampire.

CANCER RISING *Passive-aggressive Vampire, given to falling in love with your victims. Think Edward Cullen.*

LEO RISING *Supermagnetic Vampire, with perfect hair and impeccable caping skills, played by Louis Jourdan in the movie in your mind.*

VIRGO RISING *A Vampire in control, with respectable clothes; Discworld's Lady Margolotta von Uberwald would be a role model.*

LIBRA RISING *Hot-yet-cool Vampire with very fine black leather coat that gives great swirl; Buffy's Angel springs to mind.*

SCORPIO DEMON *Nosferatu. Mesmerizingly terrifying. The Max Schreck boss version not the Klaus Kinski remake.*

SAGITTARIUS RISING *Rugged, rather sweaty, outdoor Vampire not a million miles from* True Blood's *Sheriff Eric Northman.*

CAPRICORN RISING *What could be a better look than the Count himself? Bela Lugosi is your man.*

AQUARIUS RISING *Steampunk Undead; Gary Oldman in the round blue glasses; or as van Helsing, just to be contrary.*

PISCES RISING *Shapeshifting Vampire; sometimes Lon Chaney, sometimes hanging from the rafters, sometimes a heap of clothes in the corner.*

Living with your monster

LIVING WITH YOUR MONSTER IS A DAILY CHALLENGE IN EVERY
SCENARIO. HERE ARE THE ANSWERS TO SOME TAURUS FAQs.

What triggers your monster?

If anyone wants to see you morph from benign ruminant to crazed gore
junkie, all they have to do is disrupt your routine, move your stuff, or steal
a French fry from your plate. You fall for it every time. I'm afraid that the
zodiac is rammed with naughty picadors for whom Taurus-baiting is a
legitimate sport and who know where to stick the needle in to goad your
vampire into action. The transition is slow, but unstoppable. Nor do you
forget; after all, you have an eternity. You will not let it go.

How does your vampire do in love?

It is a truth universally, etc. that vampires are sexy and you, Taurus, are ruled
by Venus, making you even hotter, but the love of a vampire, as many a
virgin has discovered, is a very draining experience. It does not take much
to get you out of your casket: if your lover raises an eyebrow when you
choose their clothes, order for them in a restaurant, give them presents they
don't want (such as a GPS-enabled laptop so that you always know where
they are) you move in closer, suck away their life blood, and their will to
live. A lover who shows any interest in another being, human or otherwise,
gets locked in your well-appointed dungeon. If you are a Taurus male, you
know that you have the words Meal Ticket branded on your backside, which
means you call the tune; if you are a Taurus female, you want to wear the
leather pants. Either way it's all about possession and control. Delicious.

What does your vampire do at work?

Unless they are the Cullens, vampires spend the daylight hours asleep in
their coffins. This is pretty much your ideal job. Whatever you actually

do, as long as it is the same every day, the vampire sleeps through unless
(a) meetings are rescheduled without six months notice, (b) the vending
machine is empty, (c) a new-broom CEO introduced flexi-time or walking
meetings, (d) your desk is moved, or (e) someone uses your special mug.
Your vampire emerges, doubly murderous because its routine has been
disrupted. You go for the throat and bleed your enemies dry, metaphorically
speaking (although not always).

How can you tame your monster?

Self-examination is not a preoccupation of yours, so you rarely return from
a rampage crippled by guilt. Your rules are clear, and if people overstep
the line and incur your wrath, they have no one to blame but themselves.
Listen up, dumb kids who think it's a great idea to shelter from the storm
in a ruined castle in the middle of nowhere. But your insurance premiums
are astronomical and the injunctions are piling up, so you have to rein
yourself in. When the fangs start to throb, try counting things. Your money,
for instance. For practical day-to-day control, always carry a chocolate bar
or three; break off the squares, and count them before eating.

GETTING PROTECTION

*What can the rest of us do to protect ourselves from your
bloodlust? Traditionally, Vampires are repelled by sunlight, holy
water, crucifixes, garlic, and stakes. The righteous fire of holy water
may not have much of an effect on your thick hide; the mention of
a stake may confuse you, at least until you had grasped the concept
of homonym. A crucifix? You're likely to whip out your eyeglass
and point out that it's not silver. We could hold up a mirror (Venus
loves mirrors) and hide while you are ruminating about why you
can't see yourself. Garlic is the safest bet. You'd either be repelled or
you would stop rampaging to go and find your favorite aïoli recipe.
Either way, we could run and wait until dawn and safety.*

GEMINI

Gemini the Twins • May 22–June 21 • Mutable Air Sign
• Positive Sign • Ruled by: Mercury

You Jekyll...

Aw, we love you almost as much as you love yourself/ves, Gemini. Charming, witty, entertaining, confident, so easy to talk to, an effortless networker, and the life and soul of the party; you always seem to be having so much fun, and we all love to stand next to you in the hope that some rubs off on us, even if it does make us look a little needy.

And there's that glint of naughtiness behind your sparkly eyes, letting us know you are a bit of a badboy; and who doesn't love a badboy (step forward Captain Jack Sparrow)? Ruled by the element of air and the planet Mercury you are the Jumping Jack Flash of the zodiac.

...you Hyde

However, Jumping Jack Flash isn't exactly Mr. Solid, and it's only a shrug and shimmy from lovable flake to high-functioning sociopath, by which I mean lying, dissembling, fast-talking, empty-hearted manipulator who melts from the scene, like Macavity when you've caused maximum mayhem and have got bored. You are the third sign of the zodiac so you can choose to be a tripod (stable) or a three-wheeled car (unstable)—one for each twin. Guess which one you go for, Gemini Hyde. Silver of tongue and light of finger, a con artist of bedazzling finesse, you maintain it's a privilege for the rest of us schmucks to be duped by you. Well, you would say that wouldn't you?

Gemini: the Poltergeist

You are a Mutable Air sign. Mutable signs are what shift the celestial energy, otherwise you'd be stuck in a changeless zodiac. Grim. They mark the end of a cycle, breaking everything down so that its atoms can be reassembled into the next one. Air is the element of the intellect, intangible, and chilly, but essential for an oxygenated universe. When skies are blue, you're thinking transformative, winds of change, going forward, and other positive although slightly vague affirmations; when skies are gray you're lost and wetting your pants in a malevolent confusing fog full of dark shadows and inexplicable chills that make your hair stand on end.

Shapeshifting; unpindownable; all in the mind maybe? Maximum effect for minimum material outlay? Contracts written on the wind that blow away and leave no evidence? Gemini, you are a spook. In the real world you may be a spy, but your inner monster is a ghost. You can carry off anything from the Woman in Black to a Scooby Gang stooge, but you are your best as a poltergeist, that's the mischief-loving one associated with adolescents and usually put down to raging hormones. (Already you got an alibi!) You are famous for being young at heart, so is it your fault if your inner monster is as well?

If you're caught (unlikely, I know), do you acknowledge your evil twin and beg for help to exorcise it? Of course not, you love your evil twin, but you're not going to pass on sitting in a room full of earnest empathetic therapists and talking brokenly of your terrible early life when you were chained in the cellar of a mansion/raised by wolves/sold in the market down in New Orleans. Watching them fall for it doubles the fun.

Who you gonna call?

So how do you manifest?

Well you don't; you are a ghost, duh. Ghosts are invisible and we will only know you by your works, just like we can only know what dark matter is all about by looking at the behavior of perfectly visible matter around it. You could have fun juggling with ectoplasm, but it's even more fun to go commando. You simply fade into the background (which should be a bit of a clue as you are usually the center of an adoring crowd) and bad things start happening. You know, little things like money and smartphones disappearing, stuff flying through the air and getting inexplicably smashed up, cars moving ALL BY THEMSELVES in the middle of the night, perfectly tidy rooms turned into tsunami wrecks in a nanosecond, the family computer trashed. And that's when you are only slightly miffed. If you are feeling extra evil, you mess with our heads, mongering rumors, spreading disinformation, breathing anonymous whispers on the wind. And when we are red-eyed from sleepless nights of anxiety, you are there to charm and console, and cackle inwardly at our destabilization. Double treat.

[For other ghosts in the zodiac see Libra and Aquarius]

Other Evil Influences

IT'S ALWAYS USEFUL TO HAVE OTHERS AROUND, SOMETHING ELSE ONTO
WHICH YOU CAN SEAMLESSLY SHIFT ANY BLAME; HOW YOU EXPRESS YOUR
SPECTRAL STYLE IS INFLUENCED BY OTHER ZODIACAL HAPPENINGS; YOUR
RULING PLANET, WHERE YOUR MOON IS LURKING, AND WHAT SIGN WAS
OOZING OVER THE EASTERN HORIZON AT THE TIME OF YOUR BIRTH.

Bad moon

Your Moon expresses the Inner You. In your case, Gemini, there are two Inner Yous
and as boundaries mean nothing to you, it's not always easy to tell the Inner Yous
from your outer selves. Keep the punters confused. Your Moon can be placed in any
of the zodiac houses when you are born and modify your monster (although not
in a good way, of course). Here's how it affects the Gemini Ghost.

MOON IN ARIES *Barbecue Poltergeist: the
one that fans the flames, burns the burgers, loses
the tongs, and sears the cook.*
MOON IN TAURUS *Luxury-loving
Poltergeist: the original bull in the china store.*
MOON IN GEMINI *Professional Poltergeist:
used by the CIA as cover after they have trashed
properties during an illegal search.*
MOON IN CANCER *Kitchen Poltergeist: the
one who smashes plates, burns pans, and drops
the best knife into the waste disposal.*
MOON IN LEO *Theatrical Poltergeist: the
phantom of the opera without the singing.*
MOON IN VIRGO *Reverse Poltergeist: the
kind that tidies, leaving a teen's bedroom looking
worryingly pristine.*

MOON IN LIBRA *Vanity Poltergeist: the one
who rigs the scales to make us fat.*
MOON IN SCORPIO *Creepy Poltergeist: the
one who moves things very slightly, so that we
begin to doubt our sanity.*
MOON IN SAGITTARIUS *Autopoltergeist:
the one who blows up the radiator out of cell
range on a desert road trip.*
MOON IN CAPRICORN *Financial Poltergeist:
haunts ATMs and chews up cash cards at Christmas,
Thanksgiving, and when we are out of gas.*
MOON IN AQUARIUS *Techno Poltergeist: the
one that incites machines into revolt.*
MOON IN PISCES *Drinker's Poltergeist; why
those bottles that were half full when we went to
bed are empty this morning.*

How does your planet bring out your ghost?

It's an inexhaustible source of twanging nervous energy—what are ghosts but vibrations on another plane, eh?—and moving fast while seemingly standing still. Gemini is ruled by Mercury, an interfering multitasker after your own black heart, who has a night shift wrangling Virgo. It's named for the messenger of the Roman gods—what an opportunity to stir up trouble on Parnassus with just a bit of miscommunication!

What's that coming over the hill?

The sign rising over the eastern horizon when you were spawned represents your public persona, your outer appearance; in this case, what kind of Ghost you might look like when possessed, or how you would secretly like to manifest in the real world if only you could.

ARIES RISING *We can't see you, but the scorchmarks and the smell of burned carpet are a giveaway.*

TAURUS RISING *We can almost see you, a patch of thicker air hovering like a predator over the dessert cart.*

GEMINI RISING *We can't see either of you, which is exactly the way all four of you like it.*

CANCER RISING *We can sometimes see you far off, in a very faint outline under the glare of a full moon.*

LEO RISING *We can't see you, but the air around where you should be throbs and sparkles like malfunctioning Christmas lights.*

VIRGO RISING *We can't see you, only the pattern your finger draws in the dust on the windowsill.*

LIBRA RISING *We can't see you, which is our loss, but unfortunately there's nothing you can do about it.*

SCORPIO RISING *We can't see you, but there's an inexplicable patch of darker darkness under the bed.*

SAGITTARIUS RISING *We can see you right on the edge of vision, St. Elmo's fire crackling around your arrow tips.*

CAPRICORN RISING *We can't see you, but there is a lingering goaty aroma.*

AQUARIUS RISING *We can't see you, but if we follow the cat's eyeline we'll know where you are.*

PISCES RISING *We can't see you, but there's broken glass and damp, ghostly paw prints to show where you've been.*

Living with your monster

LIVING WITH YOUR MONSTER IS A DAILY CHALLENGE IN EVERY SCENARIO. HERE ARE THE ANSWERS TO SOME GEMINI FAQS.

What triggers your monster?

Being outsmarted (although this is statistically very unlikely, and only happens when you are incapacitated by the common cold, or pneumonic plague as you called it when you called in sick on the day of the big game). Boredom. Other people being tediously dull and following the rules. Standing still for long periods. Look, you just go ghost when you feel like it. Ghosts aren't tied to a dawn-to-dusk/full moon/waiting to be summoned schedule, they just apparate whenever they please.

How does your ghost do in love?

You know when lovers complain that their beloved just isn't there for them? That would be you. Once you have made them scream (with delight) you evaporate, become nothing more than a voice in the ether, making yourself even more desirable, of course. As you rarely listen to anything your lovers say, or care what they do, not much gets your ghost unless they (a) propose, (b) invite you to dinner with mom and dad, (c) don't invite you to the VIP red carpet do they are organizing. But your biggest trigger is rabid FOMO (fear of missing out). How could you solidify into just the two steady relationships when there are so many others out there? If you are a Gemini male you are the irresistible bad hat who drifts in and out of lovers' lives. If you are a Gemini female, ditto. You've never reckoned much to rigid gender demarcation.

What does your ghost do at work?

Most jobs come easy to you, but you don't let on, because you use all your spare time to cause misery and mayhem, by stealth. You may have your dream job as a spy, private eye, art scholarship funded situationist prankster, or you may be slumming it in a call center in Dullsville, there doesn't need to be any trigger, apart from maybe your boss's smug face. When you see a loophole, a blackmail opportunity, something incriminating left in the printer tray, or spat out by a malfunctioning shredder, you use it. No one will know it's you because you are the ghost in plain sight. On a quiet day, you troll the intranet, misforward emails, tattle in the washroom, spin by the watercooler not because of any animus, but for the unholy fun of it.

How can you tame your monster?

Why would you want to? It's your greatest asset. If people can't smell a scam or call ghostbusters, is that your fault? And anyway it's a service to society, duller people love to have the bejasus scared out of them. It's not like you are wrestling with your Darkside. You know you are behaving badly; you just don't care. Besides which, you never get caught. Well, hardly ever, and even if you do, you can blame your other twin. If ever cornered, by a team of SWAT paranormalists maybe, you pull the timeless Gemini double bluff maneuver: 'fess up prettily, and swear never to do it again unless invited to a Caspar the Friendly Ghost themed party. You are lying, of, course, but punters only see and hear what they want.

GETTING PROTECTION

What can the rest of us do to protect ourselves from you and your sly spookiness? Apparently Ghosts can be repelled by hagstones made from chalcedony and onyx, but I have a strong suspicion you'd palm them and get them fenced before we could say begone, foul fiend. We could take the bell, book, and candle exorcism approach, but you'd just ring the bell, trash the book, and blow out the candle. We could stick together; there's safety in numbers, but you love a crowd. It makes it easier to pick pockets with your little light fingers (Gemini rules the hands) and slip away undetected. That leaves the traditional blanket-over-the-head solution; corny, I know, and gives us bad hair, but at least it will muffle your persuasive sales patter.

CANCER

Cancer the Crab • June 21–July 22 • Cardinal Water Sign
• Negative Sign • Ruled by: Moon

You Jekyll...

*You'd really rather the rest of the zodiac didn't look at you,
after all it's only you, and you much prefer scuttling sideways
through the world in cozy Kevlar carapace doing good by
stealth, extending the helping claw, whether asked to or not.*

*Cancer is the fourth sign of the zodiac, carrying everyone's
emotional baggage and the picnic basket (you don't mind,
really you don't), ruled by the element water and the Moon.
When the rest of us have fallen off life's merry-go-round who
do we turn to? Cancer the caring Crab, an inexhaustible
source of empathy/sympathy, ready to put yourself on hold
while you bake us a cake or scrub our little tearstained cheeks,
and make us feel as if we've come home to mom.*

...you Hyde

Momness is a double-edged cookie cutter. Remember
what happened to Norman Bates? A traditional method
(you love the old ways) of controlling without having
to confront, it provides plenty of solid self-martyring
opportunities. You start your journey into darkness
by getting miffed about people Not Appreciating all
you've done for them even though they didn't know it,
and didn't want it done. Soon you escalate into full-on
grudge harboring, which is your favorite thing next to
existential despair, mood swings, and worrying about
things you can do nothing about; if you can point out
the cloud inside every silver lining and sprinkle some
gloom dust as you go, your work is done.

The Weremom

You are a Cardinal Water sign. Cardinal signs, as we have seen, are the boss or quintessence of their element. Water is the element of emotion, sensitivity, and feelings, including those of the gut kind (Cancer rules the breast and stomach). You are sitting in your very own bottomless rockpool of the stuff. On the slightly less gloomy side this means that your well of compassion will never run dry; on the actual gloomy side, it means there can be no end to your suffering, or that of all those within complaining distance of you when you are baying at the moon in your infinite and unstoppable melancholy.

In thrall to the Moon, addicted to lonely howling, a sucker for suffering, a martyr to mood swings that seem beyond your control, monthly cravings for food you just shouldn't go near—werewolf! D'ya think? Aaoooh! And not just any old lycanthrope, you are the mother wolf, maker of other werewolves. Don't go all faux modest now. Family is everything; and we all know how you can turn a partyful of happy extraverts into an alienated assembly of self-doubters when you're in full Eeyore mode. As lupine loping is not easily done sideways, you often get caught and have learned not to stray far from home when the Moon is Full, which is why your nearest and dearest are the ones most likely to get torn to shreds.

Of course, when you wake up in the forest clearing with nothing but a hair shirt and self-inflicted scars, you feel mortified. Exquisitely mortified. In fact this is the bit you like best. Remorse and angst flood your soul as recollection creeps back, but you secretly adore writhing around in this kind of delicious moral stew (and I know this is true because I'm one of you).

So how do you manifest?

It's not instant and it's rather uncomfortable to watch as you struggle out of your shell and into the wolf suit, but you are at least predictable. It will be about once a month, which may or may not coincide with the Full Moon; that is more of a guideline for the rest of the zodiac. After a few weeks of sucking it up, fielding perceived insults, sensing criticism of any kind, and stockpiling resentment at how underappreciated you are, the dam bursts and you go postal. The first sign is the tightening of the martyred little smile and the slipping of the brave face. That vertical groove you have between your eyebrows gets deeper. Your jaw sticks out. You start wishing you had retractable claws like Wolverine. Then you lose it and fall savagely on random innocent bystanders in revenge for a cutting remark someone completely different made to you weeks ago. After the wolf has retreated, you bitterly regret the mauling, but spend so much time oppressively making it up to your victims that they would probably prefer to be just left for dead, as at least that gets it over with.

[For other werewolves in the zodiac see Scorpio and Pisces]

I see a bad moon rising...

Other Evil Influences

YOU MAY BE OLD SCHOOL, BUT NOT ALL WOLVES ARE ALIKE, EVEN IN
THE DARK; HOW YOU EXPRESS YOUR WEREWOLF STYLE IS INFLUENCED
BY OTHER ZODIACAL HAPPENINGS; YOUR RULING PLANET, WHERE YOUR
MOON IS LURKING, AND WHAT SIGN WAS OOZING OVER THE EASTERN
HORIZON AT THE TIME OF YOUR BIRTH.

Bad moon

Your Moon expresses the Inner You; as the most defensive sign of the zodiac, Cancer, most of you is inner, and you prefer it that way as you would hate anyone to find out what you really feel. Your Moon can be placed in any of the zodiac houses when you are born and modify your monster (although not in a good way, of course). Here's how it affects the Cancer Werewolf.

MOON IN ARIES *Soccer mom Werewolf, mauls the coach if the cubs don't make the first team.*

MOON IN TAURUS *Conscientious mom Werewolf, always takes a doggy bag home.*

MOON IN GEMINI *Flirty, totally hot mom Werewolf who abandons the cubs to run off with a besotted vampire.*

MOON IN CANCER *Matriarch Werewolf, leader of the pack, the Darkside Akela.*

MOON IN LEO *Queen momma Werewolf, direct descendant of the wolf that suckled Romulus and Remus, the founders of Rome.*

MOON IN VIRGO *Practical mom Werewolf who always remembers to pack the bandages and spare underwear.*

MOON IN LIBRA *Airhead mom Werewolf who often fails to transform as she cannot decide which fur color to go with.*

MOON IN SCORPIO *Scary mom Werewolf. The cubs don't invite friends for sleepovers.*

MOON IN SAGITTARIUS *Action mom Werewolf, leaves the cubs home alone to go transforming in faraway places.*

MOON IN CAPRICORN *Career mom Werewolf, signs the cubs on as unpaid interns.*

MOON IN AQUARIUS *Eccentric mom Werewolf, embarrasses the cubs by transforming in the checkout line as if no one's looking.*

MOON IN PISCES *Guilt-tripping mom Werewolf, you could have been a fox; it's all the fault of those pesky cubs.*

How does your planet bring out your werewolf?

Chains you to the mood swing treadmill using nothing but phases and tidal power; Cancer is ruled by the Moon, which is not a planet but a lump of rock living on borrowed light. It makes up for this by sticking so close to Earth that it's always visible even when it isn't. It has no proper name, just like Mom doesn't, three goddesses work under it; yours is Diana, goddess of childbirth and sudden death, who hunts by the Full Moon.

What's that coming over the hill?

The sign rising over the eastern horizon when you were spawned represents your public persona, your outer appearance; in this case, what kind of Werewolf you might look like when transformed, or how you would like to manifest in the real world if only you could.

ARIES RISING *Ginger blood-clotted fur, red eyes, broken claws, a stranger to the grooming parlor; a hint of mutt.*

TAURUS RISING *Chocolate fur, orange eyes, Chanel Rouge Noir on the claw tips, protective leather basque; a hint of boxer.*

GEMINI RISING *Brindled fur, yellow-flecked eyes, French manicure, long and lean like you were before the cubs; a hint of greyhound.*

CANCER RISING *Last year's fur (shabby but still serviceable), silver eyes, neglected claws (you're not worth it); a hint of collie.*

LEO RISING *Glossy golden fur, golden eyes, ruby claw varnish, a less well-bred transforming buddy; almost entirely afghan.*

VIRGO RISING *Trim brown fur, navy blue eyes, perfect claws, fresh from bathtime; a hint of poodle crossed with a Siamese cat.*

LIBRA RISING *Ash blonde fur with ghostly markings, opal eyes, pearlized claws, minimal panting; a hint of golden retriever.*

SCORPIO RISING *Matte black fur, black eyes, black steel-tipped claws, own muzzle for self control; a hint of dobermann.*

SAGITTARIUS RISING *Mud-clotted fur, purple eyes, ragged claws, brings own Frisbee, uncontrollable tail wagging; almost entirely labrador*

CAPRICORN RISING *Gray fur, gray eyes, immaculate claws, collar pouch for business cards (Lycanthropy, Inc); a hint of terrier.*

AQUARIUS RISING *Striped fur, kaleidoscope eyes, bionic claws, flickers with static electricity; the Hound of the Baskervilles with a hint of basenji.*

PISCES RISING *Damp shaggy fur, glassy eyes, bitten claws, carries own brandy barrel on collar; a hint of puli.*

Living with your monster

LIVING WITH YOUR MONSTER IS A DAILY CHALLENGE IN EVERY
SCENARIO. HERE ARE THE ANSWERS TO SOME CANCER FAQS.

What triggers your monster?

Well, who would know except you, because if a person can't see that
they have wounded you, you sure ain't going to tell them. Some of us are
proactive; you are propassive. It'll be a nano thing that no one else could
remember, except another Cancerian, that flips you out of your default
mode (constant low level tetch) into a howling rage, but usually in another
room where no one can see you because even when the wolf has you, your
soul remembers that you are really a crab, and you hate being looked at.

How does your werewolf do in love?

Where would pulp romance be without a terrible hidden secret and a lover
who plays hard to get, eh? Your wolf howls when the love object (a) forgets
the anniversary of your first row, (b) refuses a third wedge of your home-
built cheesecake, (c) whistles merrily through one of your long moody
silences, (d) does not need your help in any way, or (e) is smart, solvent,
in the same time zone, and actually likes you. After a night of rampaging
passion, which they enjoy and so do you, very secretly, you're the one
silently stitching up the slashes in your T-shirt feeling gratifyingly bad
about yourself. If you are a Cancer male, you're the strong, silent stereotype,
and women long to unlock the secrets of your soul; if you are a Cancer
female, you are the old-fashioned girl who men take home to meet their
moms, who know all about the wolf, and hate you.

What does your werewolf do at work?

The Cancerian wolf is a shy creature and few workmates have witnessed
your transformation from mild-mannered self-negating people pleaser to

a feral beast in an ill-fitting garment. You could have a whole career, get a retirement watch and everything, and no one would know. This is because (a) you are usually triggered by an event in your previous job—they preferred store cookies to your homemade ones, you staggered under a mismanaged workload because you never confronted your line manager, you were underappreciated; (b) you only ever hit the night shift (you need a Moon), and (c) always clean up the blood-soaked boardroom before anyone gets in—it's a thankless task, but someone's got to do it.

How can you tame your monster?

Oh, that you could, you would love to, but 'tis is an ancient curse, wished upon your ancestral clan after The Great Betrayal of 1492; it is your duty to bear it so that others don't have to; besides, you secretly like it—there's only so much selfless caring a crab can do and after weeks with the empathy button on 11, running wild and shell-free is pant-wettingly glorious. If your secret has got out, and the vampires are gathering, try homeopathic micro-rages to let off steam; or keep a mood dairy and when you feel the hair growing, stuff yourself comatose with carbs and cream. They'll call it emotional eating. Little do they know.

GETTING PROTECTION

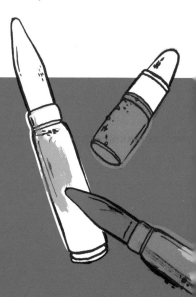

As the only recorded effective antiwerewolf potion was decocted by Severus Snape and is NOT REAL, we are at a bit of a loss here. Traditionally it is the silver bullet (which stops your heart, but then whose wouldn't it?), vampire venom (hard to get and the cure is often worse than affliction), beheading (the whole wolf/axe/ woodcutter thing is attractively traditional, but we would have to explain later at the precinct). Kinder to keep our lunar calendars updated and cage you up at the critical period, which might work if we presented it as a pamper day at a high-security rehab spa. In extremis, we could throw food and run away. You can't bear waste, and we'll get a head start while you eat it up.

LEO

Leo the Lion • July 23–August 22 • Fixed Fire Sign
• Positive Sign • Ruled by: The Sun

You Jekyll...

In public you are one big pussycat: attractive, generous, comfortable in your skin, a gracious boss, and happy family lion. Oozing confidence as you stroll down the sunny side of the street, you wrap the rest of us in the security blanket of your radiant self-belief; we know everything is fine because you're in charge, and you wouldn't have it any other way.

Leo is the fifth sign of the zodiac, a heartbeat to the left of center stage; you don't care to look undignified and pushy. Besides, you need an entourage, and an acolyte or two ahead of you to strew the rose petals. You're ruled by the Sun, the epicenter of the solar system, and the element of Fire, creator and destroyer of worlds. You are the monarch of all you survey.

...you Hyde

But history (and *Star Wars*) tells us that it is a mere throne's throw from monarch to tyrant and that even the noblest Jedi Knight can go over to the Darkside. You may spend a lot of time looking beneficently gorgeous and purring when stroked, but you are, well, you know, a lion, king of the jungle, etc., and when your divine rights are threatened, or courtiers get uppity, you flash the claws, bare the teeth, and roar, unleashing the despotic evil emperor within; and order a minion to scratch out the eyes of the offender, as you don't demean yourself with the little people. What is the point of being an alpha carnivore if you can't draw blood now and again?

Leo: the Demon King

You are a Fixed Fire sign. Fire is energy, creativity, a life force (we'll play down the death force aspect). In the drama that's your life, you see yourself as Prometheus, you know, the Titan who stole fire from the gods and gave it to humanity, thus becoming the Great Benefactor. It ended badly, but we all remember your name. Fixed signs keep everything in order, preserve the status quo: status, a word after your own heart. So, gathered around a cozy hearth, all shadows and terror kept outside the magic circle of your royal presence, we are toasty and warm; but when you roar the flames into a raging inferno that consumes us, we are simply toast.

What kind of monster would give you the dramatic scope to explore your hideous side? Got to be the Demon King, what else? You're hardly going to get off the lounger to be the Demon of Small Things, now are you? It's not so much choice, more Dynastic Imperative; your Duty. Why else have you got a crown-size groove in your head and an unshakeable sense of unearned entitlement? It's got to be the whole deal—oversize horns, rod of power, iron crown, crimson cape, your moves suffused by the red glow of eternal flames, groveling minions…and your own dressing room.

After a Demon King's scenery-devouring performance, are you contrite? Hell no. Never apologize; never explain. Righteous anger deserves righteous expression and you can't be angry any other way, as you're never wrong. Anything that happens when you're channeling the Demon King is legitimate, you have no responsibility, the role is bigger than the actor. You could blame the heavy weight of kingship taking its toll, but that would be you trying out a new bit of stagecraft: pathos with dignity, darling.

I am the king of hellfire.

So how do you manifest?

In a blaze of glory, how else? What is the point of manifesting as a wispy sheet of ectoplasm under a dark ouija board where no one can see you? Subtlety is for little monsters. Your manifestations are the hottest ticket in town. If your agent wasn't a spineless schmoe there'd be sheet lightning, thunderclaps, sulfur clouds, dry ice, a trapdoor, even…but you are a trooper, you can do without props. You turn your back on trembling offenders, get into character, and suddenly you are two feet taller with rolling eyes, gnashing teeth, and flaring nostrils. You pace up and down, prowling around the stage (all your world's stage), tearing your hair (carefully), throwing your arms about wildly, swishing your tail, like Mick Jagger channeling Smaug; you may call upon the Prince of Darkness himself to witness your suffering. You don't argue, you soliloquize at 100 decibels (not SHOUTING, *projecting!*). Any witless fool who interrupts your flow with a rational explanation gets kebabed on the pitchfork of your scorn. Of course, you are utterly, utterly exhausted when it's all over, and have to be helped away by minions, like James Brown after a particularly draining rendition of *Sex Machine*.

[For other demons in the zodiac see Sagittarius and Aries]

MANY ARE THE WAYS FOR A DEMON KING TO RULE,
AND JUST HOW YOU STAMP YOUR DEMONIC AUTHORITY
ON THE UNIVERSE IS INFLUENCED BY OTHER ZODIACAL HAPPENINGS;
YOUR RULING PLANET, WHERE YOUR MOON IS LURKING, AND WHAT SIGN
WAS OOZING OVER THE EASTERN HORIZON AT THE TIME OF YOUR BIRTH.

Bad moon

Your Moon expresses the Inner You. As the Moon is a mere reflection of the Sun, from where it gets all its light, so your Inner You, Leo, is pretty much a paler, more insubstantial version of the Outer You. Your Moon can be placed in any of the zodiac houses when you are born and modify your monster (although not in a good way, of course). Here's how it affects the Leo Demon.

MOON IN ARIES *Mad, cackling extra demonic Demon King; owns the soul of Caligula.*

MOON IN TAURUS *Gluttonous, power-crazed, libidinous Demon King with private banqueting pit; owns the soul of Henry VIII.*

MOON IN GEMINI *Usurping Demon King; not really the Demon King, but his murderous twin brother; owns the soul of King John.*

MOON IN CANCER *Dynastic Demon King who wants to keep it all in the family; owns the soul of Queen Victoria.*

MOON IN LEO *Extravagant Demon King with a palace in every circle. Owns the soul of Louis XIV, the Sun King.*

MOON IN VIRGO *Fastidious Demon King; owns the soul of Elizabeth I.*

MOON IN LIBRA *Silver-tongued Demon King; owns the soul of Richard III.*

MOON IN SCORPIO *Bowel-melting Demon King. More demon tyrant really; owns the souls of all the Medici princes and Darth Vader.*

MOON IN SAGITTARIUS *Absentee Demon King, forever riding out with other demons; owns the soul of Richard the Lionheart.*

MOON IN CAPRICORN *Miserly Demon King with the keys to the treasury welded to its pitchfork; owns the soul of Henry VII.*

MOON IN AQUARIUS *Unwilling Demon King, agitating to declare hell The Glorious Demons' Infernal Republic; owns the soul of Oliver Cromwell.*

MOON IN PISCES *Fantasist Demon King; owns the soul of Ludwig II of Bavaria.*

How does your planet bring out your demon?

It confers unshakeable validation of your right to be the king of the pit. Leo is ruled by the Sun, the boss, the actual star, not just a planet, of the whole solar shebang, the one that sits in the center allowing the rest of creation to revolve around it. From afar, it beams down warmth, encouraging health, wealth and happiness, but up close it is a gigantic scary ball of gases going nuclear that will devour you whole. And it's got its own gods.

What's that coming over the hill?

The sign rising over the eastern horizon when you were spawned represents your public persona, your outer appearance; in this case, what kind of Demon King you might look like when possessed, or how you would like to manifest in the real world if you could.

ARIES RISING *Devil may care Demon King. Who could nail your hotheaded power? Brando, in* The Wild One *years.*

TAURUS RISING *Demon King. Bull. Vampire. Blood. You're thinking Robert de Niro. Who else could do it?*

GEMINI RISING *Deliciously naughty Demon King. Surely Johnny Depp won't be able to resist doubling up to play evil twins.*

CANCER RISING *Grumpy Demon King. You favor Harrison Ford, but your agent said W.C. Fields. Agent now in pit 7.*

LEO RISING *Double Demon King with extra dark charisma and great hair. A gift from you to Leonardo DiCaprio.*

VIRGO RISING *Exacting Demon King. You'll take the part yourself, thank you, no one else could possibly do it properly.*

LIBRA RISING *Metrosexual Demon King. Who could team nuanced evil with perfect tailoring and a hint of negligee? Cary Grant.*

SCORPIO RISING *Dark brooding Demon King. Daniel Day-Lewis will break all other contracts to play you. You have told him so.*

SAGITTARIUS RISING *Reckless Demon King. Got to be a genuine hellraiser. Steve McQueen! You'll be the stunt double.*

CAPRICORN RISING *Serious Demon King. It's all about money, strategic silence, and revenge Clint Eastwood would do you justice.*

AQUARIUS RISING *Alien Demon King. Back home it would be X-B!n'izt, but on Earth you'd take Dr. Spock. Or C-3P0.*

PISCES RISING *Disorderly irresponsible Demon King. Has to be your old buddy Jack Nicholson. Jack's played you lots of times.*

Living with your monster

LIVING WITH YOUR MONSTER IS A DAILY CHALLENGE IN EVERY
SCENARIO. HERE ARE THE ANSWERS TO SOME LEO FAQS.

What triggers your monster?

Being looked at from your not-best side. Bad lighting; not being given the
attention that is yours by right; insufficient admiration; lack of respect, aka
craven fawning. You resist manifesting at the opening of every available
envelope (although a Demon King's got to network), and will only accept
a summons if it's for an A-list red carpet VIP event, but sometimes you treat
your Z-listers to a full-on, all-the-stops-out show, for free, without them having
to do anything, just to see the stunned expressions on their plain little faces.

How does your demon do in love?

As the King says, you're just a hunk, a hunk o' burnin' love: ardent, amorous
(Leo rules the heart), and other A words, but you crave quantity: you are
a gift to the world, not just the One, who might get boring and cramp
your style. As long as lovers do what you say, put in the adoring hours, and
are comfortable in a crowd, it will be fine; the demon only awakes if they
(a) look better than you, (b) dress out of thrift stores, (c) upstage you on
karaoke night, (d) give you socks for your birthday, (e) want quality time
with just the two of you. You burst into flames (figuratively) and either
brand them with hot tongs so they can never love another OR banish their
souls into the everlasting torment that is life without you. If you are a Male
Leo you are a satanic rock god with an enormous rider; if you are a Female
Leo you are a diva, surrounded by etiolated and bankrupted fools.

What does your demon do at work?

Whatever the job is, you're in charge. You are a pussycat of a boss and only
release the demon when (a) people you have told to do stuff haven't done

stuff, (b) people did exactly what you said and now you need someone to blame, (c) you have to do your own photocopying, d) they bring you whole milk instead of skinny latte, (e) you don't get total credit for all the work you told someone to do. Who knew you could slam doors in an open plan office? I sometimes suspect, Leo, that you amp up the rage a tad more than needed, for dramatic effect.

How can you tame your monster?

Why should you? Your public adore it, and you cannot disappoint them. The show must go on, even if it means draining yourself daily belting out bravura performances full of demonic demon-ness. But maybe you are getting the vibes that Demon Kings are a bit passé as people turn to boxed set zombies for their terror fix, so you may have to redefine your role. Try workshopping the act unplugged, without an audience; aim to just growl a bit and spend a relaxing hour posting selfies on Instagram. If you're caught unawares, put your paws over your ears and hum la-la-la or your mantra of choice, and remind yourself that towering rages give you crows-feet.

GETTING PROTECTION

So how do us huddled masses protect ourselves from your scorching roar? Demons can be repelled by salt, holy water, iron, amulets, and pentacles, but they don't always know that, and Demon Kings tend to laugh hideously in the face of such pathetic human defenses. Holy water would sizzle right off you. A pentacle would work, as you rise to the challenge of a small cabaret-style stage, but only for a minute or so. Iron is common, you spit on it. Amulets in the form of jewelry are the way forward, not because you are scared of sacred stones, but because you are a sucker for bling, a rhinestone and a ruby pendant dangled before your mad red eyes may sidetrack you long enough for us to run away and hide.

VIRGO

Virgo the Virgin • August 23–September 22
• Mutable Earth Sign • Negative Sign • Ruled by: Mercury

You Jekyll...

Workaday Virgo is, like Mary Poppins, practically perfect. You're industrious, hardworking, neat, an ace organizer, clever with your hands (no shelf you put up would ever dare fall down), and always pack Rescue Remedy® and bandages whenever you go out, in case anyone falls over. You are a treasure, as you modestly remind us on quite a regular basis. You love to serve.

Virgo is ruled by the useful and practical Element Earth and Mercury, the busiest planet in the system. You are the sixth sign of the zodiac, bang in the middle, handily positioned to helpfully tell the first five signs exactly what they did wrong and the following six how to do it properly. What on earth would we do without your sleepless eye for the telling detail?

...you Hyde

The detail is where the devil lives, right? (Not that you would contemplate living with the Devil—have you seen the Eighth Circle of Hell?) While you are not devilish in the noisy, red-eyed vulgar way, living with you can be hellish, what with your obsessive deployment of the wet wipe and your readiness to critique our every move. We'd rather be scourged with scorpion tails than endure another tongue lashing about the unsatisfactory state of our sock drawers/ kitchen floor (see, you're not hot on the Big Picture.) The unwary mistake your modest downward gaze for dainty-minded reserve, but I know you are just zealously scanning the floor for specks of grime.

Virgo: the Bride of Dracula

You are a Mutable Earth sign, which doesn't sound at all monstrous, does it? Earth is the indispensable element that works almost as hard as you do: it can make pots, grow stuff, build shelters, contain rivers, and best of all, you can spend hours grading it into heaps according to size, type, geological origin, mineral content, etc. Mutable signs, as we have seen, are transformative, in a constant state of flux. On a good day this means a bumper harvest, on a bad night your fidgety perfectionism means no one can ever rest comfortably, not even in their coffins.

Out with the checklist. Obsession with earth? Check. Compulsive counting? Check. Supernatural ability to drain the blood out of any human by nagging them comatose? Check. A bit Lady Macbeth around blood? Check. Vampire—it sounds bloody, juicy, and sexy; I know (don't tell me you're not thrilled), but it's not all about the Count. Regardless of any real world orientation, Virgos tend to the Bride of Dracula side of the coffin, because you love to worship; you might also go Vanir (a sect so enslaved by neatfreakery and fearful symmetry they have no time to suck). Some of you do both, a perfect Virgo vampire storm of servility and OCD.

Doesn't going vampire make you blush with shame? It would, but your feelings are irrelevant, as what you do, you do for The Master, who inhabits a higher plane. It gives you no pleasure to eviscerate people, but the Master's need is greater; you have to make sure the blood is organic before it passes his fangs. Besides, you feel so deliciously dreadful afterward that you have to scrub yourself raw, burn your clothes, and sanitize the whole block, which is half the fun.

So how do you manifest?

There are few visual clues. Unless you are the Virgo that spends every spare minute of your allotment growing organic beet fertilized only by your ineffable smugness, you are already quite pallid (tofu 'n' wheatgrass detox on permanent replay) and your eyes a bit red (you're between remedies for your chronic pink-eye), so it's hard to tell when the Vampire is in control. I suspect this may be because it is always on a cost-conscious simmer. But a sure sign that you're going Bride is an unexplained whiff of Clorox in the air, the escalating chill factor as an icy penumbra spreads outward from the place where your soul used to be, and the tightening of our collective guts in dread (Virgo rules the intestines). The giveaway is the sound of the sniffy clearing of your throat and the flicking open your PDA, as you get ready to impale us on the barbed wire of your forensic criticism. It is possible that your impeccably researched, theoretically correct critique is over in a couple of hours (you are very thorough), but it feels like endless living death.

[For other vampires in the zodiac see Capricorn and Taurus]

Other Evil Influences

YOU STRIVE FOR CONSISTENCY BUT THE STARS DENY IT; NOT YOUR FAULT, YOUR PAPERWORK WAS FLAWLESS. HOW YOU EXPRESS YOUR VAMPIRE STYLE IS INFLUENCED BY OTHER ZODIACAL HAPPENINGS; YOUR RULING PLANET, WHERE YOUR MOON IS LURKING, AND WHAT SIGN WAS OOZING OVER THE EASTERN HORIZON AT THE TIME OF YOUR BIRTH.

Bad moon

Your Moon expresses the Inner You. You'd rather it didn't; you work hard to hide the bits of you that fear that you might not be right all the time, or that you might enjoy getting down and dirty. Your Moon can be placed in any of the zodiac houses when you are born and modify your monster (although not in a good way, of course). Here's how it affects the Virgo Vampire.

MOON IN ARIES *Demonic Bride of Dracula; often summoned at human weddings.*

MOON IN TAURUS *Complacent Bride of Dracula; you've got your Mr. Undead right there with you in the casket.*

MOON IN GEMINI *Plate-throwing Bride of Dracula, but counting the pieces afterward is an obsession you can share.*

MOON IN CANCER *Martyred Bride of Dracula, always the werewolf, never the vamp.*

MOON IN LEO *Royal Bride of Dracula; wedding shower must include solid gold caskets filled with the dust of rubies.*

MOON IN VIRGO *Double-strength Bride of Dracula, the one that makes bridesmaids do bad things with the best man.*

MOON IN LIBRA *Society Bride of Dracula; hosts a Sucking Salon every Walpurgisnacht.*

MOON IN SCORPIO *Libidinous Bride of Dracula; goes for other people's fiancés.*

MOON IN SAGITTARIUS *Action Bride of Dracula; you only said yes so that you could run with the Children of the Night.*

MOON IN CAPRICORN *Business savvy Bride of Dracula; the one who opened up Castle Bran to paying tourists/victims.*

MOON IN AQUARIUS *Rebel Bride of Dracula; the one who sunbathes, eats garlic bread, and calls herself Sandra.*

MOON IN PISCES *Gore-aholic Bride of Dracula; not to be trusted at a neck without a designated driver.*

How does your planet bring out your vampire?

It keeps you relentlessly fixated on detail. Virgo is ruled by Mercury, the hyperactive multitasker that also cleans up after Gemini. It's the nearest planet to the Sun—you love being an indispensable Number Two—and is named for Mercury, the god of communications, cattle, healing, shopping, and any other activity no one else could be bothered with. He also gives his name to the metal: beautiful and useful, yet heavier and more poisonous than it looks.

What's that coming over the hill?

The sign rising over the eastern horizon when you were spawned represents your public persona, your outer appearance; in this case, what kind of Vampire you might look like when possessed, or how you would like to manifest in the real world if you could.

ARIES RISING *And the Bride wore…blood red, with a hard hat, biker boots, and a bouquet of pitchforks.*

TAURUS RISING *And the Bride wore… tight, scarlet satin and a leather choker with riding boots and a dozen black roses.*

GEMINI RISING *And the Bride wore… camouflage fatigues, stilettos, and an invisibility cloak for two.*

CANCER RISING *And the Bride wore…the same shabby dress, a flour-covered apron, and glass slippers.*

LEO RISING *And the Bride wore…a gold lurex catsuit with a black, rhinestone tiara, and a long, red veil.*

VIRGO RISING *And the Bride wore…a taupe, two piece with matching shoes; you can't be doing with expensive frippery.*

LIBRA RISING *And the Bride wore… something borrowed from Vera Wang, with bloodstone earrings made from real blood.*

SCORPIO RISING *And the Bride wore… matte black, with a cape of sable wolfskin and a single stem of belladonna.*

SAGITTARIUS RISING *And the Bride wore …surf pants, Adidas, and a Freddie Krueger fright mask. Boo!*

CAPRICORN RISING *And the Bride wore a traditional (rented) meringue with a long black veil and a bouquet of blood orange blossom.*

AQUARIUS RISING *And the Bride wore… a kilt, pool shoes, and a flying helmet; you get it so wrong sometimes.*

PISCES RISING *And the Bride wore… whatever she got up in, with ruby slippers and a bouquet of dead flowers.*

Living with your monster

LIVING WITH YOUR MONSTER IS A DAILY CHALLENGE IN EVERY
SCENARIO. HERE ARE THE ANSWERS TO SOME VIRGO FAQS.

What triggers your monster?

You know what? It may be quicker to list what doesn't: flood, plague, social
collapse, incoming asteroid, polar ice caps melting, California sliding into the
sea, your block burning down, the Four Horsemen on the doorstep (unless
one of them leaves hoofprints). Catastrophe deactivates your vampiric circuitry.
Otherwise, the Bride is a light sleeper and can be woken by anything the rest
of us try to rise above: sloppy lane discipline, books not in alphabetical order on
the shelves, a nanostain on the inside of your coveralls that no one can see…

How does your vampire do in love?

You're a Bride of Dracula, you should be beating them off with a stick
(or a stake?). You've got the whole seductive ice maiden thing going, so
where does it all go wrong? Do you want to talk about it? Well, yes you
do; you always want to talk about it. When the Besotted One (a) buys
inorganic candy, (b) proposes on the wrong knee, (c) doesn't do anything
the way you told them; (d) gets inexplicably upset because you have
thrown away their fast food menus, told them how big their butt looks in
that, or filed their IRS form for them, then you go critical and analyze The
Relationship until it is nothing but a bloodless husk which you can then
recycle as fertilizer. If you are a Virgo male, women take out restraining
orders against you; if you are a Virgo female, men want to stop you making
them over.

What does your vampire do at work?

You do all your bloodsucking at work, because (a) it's where you spend
most of your time (you haven't brought in a foldaway coffin with your

special earth in it, but I'm guessing you've got a whole bunch of house plants in your cubicle) and (b) it's a reliably constant source of minor irritation. Shoddy filing, corrupted databases, illegal cookie rustling, the wrong sort of pencils, parking lot misallocations; your vampire need never sleep. There's not much to see, because you attack by email, memo, minutes of the last meeting, phone calls, tweets, and miles and miles of blood red tape. Lifeblood drains out through papercuts. Victims lose the will to live and impale themselves on their own flash drives instead.

How can you tame your monster?

Should you though? It's your duty to tell people like it is, at fang point, even if it pains you (although it doesn't). It is For Their Own Good. Anyway, it's out of your hands, your powers are derived from a Higher Plane, who are you to argue? Consider your health. Rich blood plays havoc with your digestive system. Perhaps the Bride should be discouraged. Avoid talking cures: the temptation to tell everyone where they're going wrong will be overwhelming. For everyday control, carry a bag of organic chickpeas to count when you feel yourself slipping; playing Bejeweled should divert you in an emergency.

GETTING PROTECTION

What can the rest of us do to save ourselves from being bled dry? Traditionally, Vampires are repelled by sunlight, crucifixes, garlic, the stake, and holy water. As you wouldn't step out without SPF 70, sunlight doesn't phase you. Bling, however cruciform it is, will not impress you much either, and you grow your own organic garlic, thank you. If we came at you with a stake, you'd have it covered in plastic wrap before the point scraped breastbone. Perhaps we could hold up a picture of a pointilliste meisterwerk which would frazzle you by being both the big picture AND a mass of fascinating detail? Or just spill holy water on your desk and slink away while you mop up and agonize over unsightly watermarks.

LIBRA

Libra the Scales • September 23–October 22 • Cardinal Air
Sign • Positive Sign • Ruled by: Venus

You Jekyll...

No one could believe that there is anything remotely monstrous about you, Libra. You're such a lovely person. Look at you: good-looking, so refined, stylish, sophisticated (yet blessed with the common touch), always with a kind word for everybody, and a smile as big as the Ritz. Your boatloads of friends, and quite a few of your family, all adore you.

You are the seventh sign of the zodiac—lucky number seven, such a harmonious number. Seven Heavenly Virtues, Seven Deadly Sins—balance, you see? You are ruled by Air and Venus, planet of beauty and harmony. And you do seem to belong on some other way more beautiful planet than us; you're just too good to be true.

...you Hyde

Yeah right, too good to be true; what did our mamas tell us? If something seems too good to be true, it probably is. Look out for strings. Behind the wall of charm, the wheels whiz around as you calculate how to nudge, nip, and tuck to tweak things to your best advantage like the Sultan of Spin you are. You are the zodiac's Cheshire Cat, nothing but a big cheesy smile that takes our money and fades away on the air while we think we are playing a flirty game of hide and seek. On the one hand you're a manipulative untrustworthy narcissist, but on the other, you're an irresistible flirtatious charmer. It's all about balance.

Libra: Ghost

You are a Cardinal Air sign. Cardinal signs are the trending fashion leaders of the zodiacal salon, dictating next season's shapes. And Air is essential—it's no life without the oxygen of publicity. Air was formed by the Earth's spin generating a magnetic field to pull in passing unwary gases (carbon dioxide, oxygen, and even the big cool one, nitrogen) to dance attendance around itself, and make life bearable. When everything is going your way, Libra, as it so often does, the universe is bright, sparkly, with room to twirl; when your charm is on the blink, the atmosphere curdles and we lumber about like gorillas in the mist.

Elusive, ethereal, patchy, and inconsistent, a triumph of style over substance—Libra you're a ghost, balancing the joy of being ultrascary while not getting all hideous and sweaty yourself. Never comfortable with just one look, one night you might channel Patrick Swayze in the movie named after you, the next just go will-o'-the-wisp for a casual, dressed-down haunting. I'm thinking your favorite has got to be the headless lady, drifting about a beautiful chunk of medieval real estate dressed in a breathtaking floaty white gown accessorized with the merest blush of bloodspatter, and your head tucked safely underneath your arm.

Do you go red with shame after a haunting at the thought of what you've done? You know, luring people out onto treacherous marshy ground and leaving them to drown? Giving portly old oil barons heart attacks? That sort of thing? This is a joke, right? No, you don't need help out of denial. You had a very happy upbringing manipulating your parents and carers by stealth, and you aren't going to stop now.

I'm always touched by your presence, dear.

So how do you manifest?

Stylishly. And often. You don't manifest spontaneously; nothing you do is spontaneous; it's all calculated. Where would you be if you let emotion get the better of you? The trick is to behave like a girly girl with a little pink mind apparently stuffed with kittens and chocolate, even when you're a boy—you are the zodiac's cross-dresser after all—but think like a monochrome forensic accountant. This is what street magicians call misdirection. Yet there is a dilemma. On the one hand, you long to manifest full-on so that everyone can see you and be enthralled by your awesomeness. On the other, that would be giving the game away and jeopardizing long-term goals. Your accountant says go invisible, but you are just that little bit too vain, so there is always the trace of a shimmering shape left in the air, or a sourceless trail of evocative perfume (or stench, if you're in a foul mood). No one will be ever be able to pin it on you, not while you control the scales of justice.

[For other ghosts in the zodiac see Aquarius and Gemini]

Other Evil Influences

YOU HATE BEING STUCK IN THE SAME SHABBY DRESS, SO IT'S GREAT THAT THE UNIVERSE OFFERS SO MANY LOOKS TO TRY ON; HOW YOU EXPRESS YOUR SPECTRAL ÉLAN IS INFLUENCED BY OTHER ZODIACAL HAPPENINGS: YOUR RULING PLANET, WHERE YOUR MOON IS LURKING, AND WHAT SIGN WAS OOZING OVER THE EASTERN HORIZON AT THE TIME OF YOUR BIRTH.

Bad moon

Your Moon expresses the Inner You. Outer You may be an airhead, but Inner You is the bookkeeper, massaging the figures to balance in your favor. What kind of books you keep depends on the Moon. Your Moon can be placed in any of the zodiac houses when you were born and modify your monster (although not in a good way, of course). Here's how it affects the Libra Ghost.

MOON IN ARIES *Headless Ghost; very popular with historical reenactment societies and amateur dramatics.*

MOON IN TAURUS *Gourmet Ghost who lives in artisan chocolate boxes and inhales all the champagne truffles.*

MOON IN GEMINI *Fashionable Ghost with a pet poltergeist, haunts Tiffany's to throw a better class of rock.*

MOON IN CANCER *Moaning Ghost that lurks inside hills and prefers to be heard not seen.*

MOON IN LEO *Aristocratic Ghost of dead royals, especially the younger, prettier ones.*

MOON IN VIRGO *Immaculate Ghost; scares people to death for their own good but doesn't leave a mark on them.*

MOON IN LIBRA *Ultratransparent Ghost, haunts mirrors and designer store fronts.*

MOON IN SCORPIO *Obsessed Ghost, haunts dark ramparts in Scandinavian castles looking for someone to avenge their death.*

MOON IN SAGITTARIUS *Prankster Ghost; likes to spook racehorses in mid-jump and dogs in the middle of the night.*

MOON IN CAPRICORN *Traditional Ghost, will only haunt ruined castles, ruined stately homes, and ruined corporate banks.*

MOON IN AQUARIUS *Snarky Ghost, haunts ghost trains for postmodern ironic fun.*

MOON IN PISCES *Unreliable Ghost, forced to wear rattling chains by other ghosts so that they know which bar it's in.*

How does your planet bring out your ghost?

Leads by example: beautiful, untouchable, wreathed in swirly, creamy mists, and spins backward on its axis, like Regan's head in *The Exorcist*. Libra is ruled by Venus, named for the goddess of Love and Negotiable Affection, the one who started up a whole war to establish who was the fairest of them all. You have to share it with Taurus, but they are vampires, dust beneath your wheels.

What's that coming over the hill?

The sign rising over the eastern horizon when you were spawned represents your public persona, your outer appearance; in this case, what kind of Ghost you might look like when possessed, or how you would secretly like to manifest in the real world if only you could.

ARIES RISING *Unfortunately, we can't see you, but you are ram shaped and ride with the Hell's Angels.*

TAURUS RISING *Unfortunately, we can't see you, but you are bull-shaped and carrying ghostly gold bars in a ghostly Louis Vuitton bucket bag.*

GEMINI RISING *Unfortunately, we can't see you, but you have split yourself in two and are now twice as scary.*

CANCER RISING *Unfortunately, we can't see you, but you are crab-shaped, and gliding silently sideways along Malibu beach.*

LEO RISING *Unfortunately, we can't see you, but you are lion-shaped and hogging the limelight.*

VIRGO RISING *Unfortunately, we can't see you, but you are the shape of a respectable young lady with a lamp.*

LIBRA RISING *Unfortunately, we can't see you, but you are even more terribly beautiful than we could possibly imagine.*

SCORPIO RISING *Unfortunately, we can't see you, but you are scorpion-shaped and dance alone on the desert's black sand.*

SAGITTARIUS RISING *Unfortunately, we can't see you, but you are centaur-shaped and winning the Kentucky Derby by a neck.*

CAPRICORN RISING *Unfortunately, we can't see you, but you are goat-shaped and eating incriminating paperwork in the boardroom.*

AQUARIUS RISING *Unfortunately, we can't see you, but you look like a man carrying water in a bucket, but it's really champagne.*

PISCES RISING *Unfortunately, we can't see you, but you are mermaid-shaped (you couldn't face fish) and luring sailors to their doom.*

Living with your monster

What triggers your monster?

No Libran would let themselves be ambushed by such a crude device as a trigger. You appear when you choose, and if you think it's not worth your while manifesting, you don't, which gives you a rep for inconsistency, patchy performance, and slothfulness. The nearest you come to it is when you feel forced to rebalance the universe, which sounds uncharacteristically superhero, but means that sometimes you bat for the angels and sometimes you're found in bed with Beelzebub, and are accused of inconsistency, again. (Like you care.)

How does your ghost do in love?

Commitmentphobia. You wrote the book, or at least dictated it to your lovely assistant. It's not that you don't love all your lovers (of course, you don't), but that you can never decide which one would serve you best, so, end up rejecting them all, and starting over. This is where your Ghost comes in handy. In ghost mode, you have perfected the art of drifting away, becoming insubstantial, fading into nothing but a dream they once had (or nightmare if it went wrong). They are ditched but amazingly don't blame you, and you can drift back into their lives again if they suddenly become richer, thinner, or more famous. Long-term goals, see? If you are a Libra male, women throw themselves at you and bounce off your charm force field. If you are a Libra female, men throw themselves and their platinum card at you, and you keep the card.

What does your ghost do at work?

Most of your work, apparently. That's your Prada jacket on the back of the chair, and your iPad flickering eerily on the desk, and there's a telltale trace of Jean-Paul Gaultier, but where are you? A one-to-one-behind closed doors with the boss maybe? Yet the reports get written, the database updated, the press releases released—that's because you have farmed them out to an adoring intern—why do you think it's called ghostwriting? Secrets and lies drift through the company like ectoplasm, generated invisibly by you. You keep the scary ghost for enemies (people who want your job or whose job you want); you whisper rumors they can't deny and manifest in the washroom mirror, undermining their confidence and sanity and in a way that they can never explain without looking dumb and getting sent on gardening leave.

How can you tame your monster?

I think we could say that you already have. It's obedient, housetrained, comes when called, and only wails on command. Ah, but your accountant may recommend that you *pretend* that you are acknowledging and taming your monster. If for some Machiavellian reason, this were the case, I'd recommend the exorcism route. There'd be incense, candles, good wine, a crowd of well wishers, you get to wear robes, and you can have a lovely party afterward.

GETTING PROTECTION

What can the rest of us do to protect ourselves from your lethal blithe spirit? Most ghost remedies are based on charms, ritual words, or a baseless belief in flower remedies because, as we instinctively know, you can't protect yourself against things that can slide through your ears and eyeballs and get inside your head. Odysseus protected himself from the sirens by being lashed to a ship's mast and stuffing his ears with wax; a tad mythic, but worth a go: maybe we could try permawearing earphones and tight jackets. I suspect that if we held up horseshoes or a bunch of parsley, you'd laugh and tickle us, and you'd sneer at the cheapskate onyx hagstone gambit (see Gemini). Diamond earrings would work though…for a while.

SCORPIO

Scorpio the Scorpion • October 23–November 22
• Fixed Water Sign • Negative Sign
• Ruled by: Pluto (and Mars, a bit)

You Jekyll...

People always seem to get a little antsy when you tell them your sun sign, Scorpio, even if they are Scorpios themselves. You can't think why. Sure, you like things your way, but who doesn't and maybe fools don't get suffered that gladly around you, but that's no reason for everyone to act like rabbits caught in the headlights. It's not very respectful of them, and you may have to sit down and have one of your little talks to find out why, exactly, they won't look you in the eye.

You are the eighth sign of the zodiac, ruled by the element of Water and the planet Pluto; you know it's been declared an ex-planet, and you're back with Mars now, but there is no way you are letting it go.

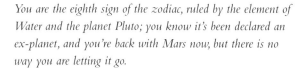

...you Hyde

Letting go is not in the Scorpio repertoire. Possession, control, and domination is your sure-fire three-step plan to master anything. There's only a thin black veil between you and your monster, although you might think we don't know that, what with you being secretive and enigmatic. Your power glare gives you away and we know what the vole feels like when it sees the eagle hovering. In the Venn diagram that represents the Hyde/Jekyll interface, your circles are almost in full eclipse, with just a tiny new-moon rind of Jekyll visible. You're already terrifying in benign mode; what fresh hell is in store when you go monster?

Scorpio: the Wolf in Wolf's Clothing

You are a Fixed Water sign. Fixed signs contain, regulate, control, keep things ominously still. The Water element is all about raw ungovernable emotion. Thank your stars that you are Fixed, then, otherwise you'd be splashing about in a maelstrom of your own self-loathing and not able to dominate anyone. When you are in control, we are looking at a dark, fathomless moonlit lake with a surface sheen as impenetrable as your eyes, and when you lose your grip, we teeter on the edge of a black fathomless abyss of stagnant water full of Things with Eyes; or an oubliette in a faraway Carpathian castle.

Triter minds would have gone for the vampire option because of the whole sex thing, but you don't do trite, you do Werewolf. After all, what are you all about? Power, instilling fear in others, relishing and controlling an insatiable sex drive (Scorpio rules the genitals). And what are werewolves all about? Power, instilling fear in others, relishing and controlling an insatiable inner beast. Some signs deny their inner monster. You own it. The regularity appeals to you (Scorpios love a routine, the more punishing the better). Your eyes go red and scary even when the Moon isn't Full; you radiate animal magnetism—and we aren't talking puppy love here.

You could say it wasn't your fault, the Moon made you do it, but you don't because you despise pretense and are contemptuous of compromise. You know perfectly well why, when the red mist recedes, everybody is cowering in the corner, immobilized in the tractor beam of your glare. They may not have been physically disemboweled and eaten alive, but it will feel like that. You would be lying if you said it didn't give you a thrill.

Let's sway under the moonlight, this serious moonlight,

So how do you manifest?

Frankly you don't look or behave that differently than your normal unnervingly controlled and enigmatically menacing self. They won't catch you skulking in a cellar with a recently defrosted chicken on a string, trying to hide your inner wolf when you can no longer keep it in. When the Scorpio Werewolf wants to manifest, you don't bother with bourgeois subterfuge; you hide in plain sight. You don't get any hairier, or fang-ier, or change shape; it's just that we get more conscious of your physicality as the air around you chills down. The worst and scariest thing is that you don't leap immediately and get it over with, as you are master of the thousand-yard icy stare, which pulverizes any shred of fight left in us (unless we are Aries, in which case the response is "bring it on, man"). It's amazing how good people are at not seeing what they are seeing, and it's a piece of cake for you to persuade them that they have not just seen you tear someone's throat out, figuratively speaking.

[For other werewolves in the zodiac see Pisces and Cancer]

Other Evil Influences

IN THE REAL WORLD YOU DON'T PERMIT OTHERS TO DILUTE YOUR POWER, BUT EVEN YOU CAN'T OUTSTARE THE STARS. HOW YOU EXPRESS YOUR WEREWOLF WILL BE INFLUENCED BY OTHER HAPPENINGS: YOUR RULING PLANET, WHERE YOUR MOON IS LURKING, AND WHAT SIGN WAS OOZING OVER THE EASTERN HORIZON AT THE TIME OF YOUR BIRTH.

Bad moon

Your Moon expresses the Inner You, even though you will it not to, as Outer You's cred in the Inquisition Chamber might evaporate if people discover Inner You's shameful cake habit and guilty-pleasure penchant for 70s' disco. Your Moon can be placed in any of the zodiac houses when you are born and modify your monster (although not in a good way, of course). Here's how it affects the Scorpio Werewolf.

MOON IN ARIES *Menacing, cold, lone Werewolf driven by a hot demon; steam from every orifice and condensation behind the eyes.*

MOON IN TAURUS *Menacing, cold, lone Werewolf with own private field for transforming purposes and roast pheasant on a string to snack on.*

MOON IN GEMINI *Menacing, cold, lone Werewolf with an unexpectedly silver tongue.*

MOON IN CANCER *Menacing, cold, lone Werewolf on the school run.*

MOON IN LEO *Menacing, cold, lone Werewolf with own Facebook page, Instagram account, and 100,500 followers on Twitter.*

MOON IN VIRGO *Menacing, cold, lone Werewolf with self-updating GPS enabled database for cross-referencing victims.*

MOON IN LIBRA *Menacing, cold, lone Werewolf secretly wearing silk under the skin.*

MOON IN SCORPIO *Extremely menacing, cold, lone Werewolf that lives only in legend.*

MOON IN SAGITTARIUS *Menacing, cold, lone Werewolf that works out and hangs with other Menacing, Cold, Lone Werewolves.*

MOON IN CAPRICORN *Menacing, cold, lone Werewolf that has turned its inner goat into a were-satyr.*

MOON IN AQUARIUS *Menacing, cold, lone Werewolf who is really the last survivor of a doomed exploratory mission from Sirius B.*

MOON IN PISCES *Menacing, cold, lone Werewolf who lures victims by pretending to have a wounded paw.*

How does your planet bring out your ghost?

Maintains your cold, icy, black broodingness and keeps your anger tanks topped off. Because you've got two planets: Pluto the furthest from earth, black, dense, frozen, mysterious, remote, and named for the god of the Underworld; and Mars, on loan from Aries, hot, red, loud, and in-your-face, named for the god of war and road rage. This makes you at once hot and cold, sexy, and aloof.

What's that coming over the hill?

The sign rising over the eastern horizon when you were spawned represents your public persona, your outer appearance; in this case, what kind of Werewolf you might look like when possessed, or how you would secretly like to manifest in the real world if only you could.

ARIES RISING *It's all in the eyes…flickering black flames and deep inside, tiny mad red dots in the shape of a fist.*

TAURUS RISING *It's all in the eyes…the color of espresso, mixed with tiny copper colored coin-shaped flecks.*

GEMINI RISING *It's all in the eyes… obscured by mirrored Ray-Bans that hide the empty soulless sockets behind.*

CANCER RISING *It's all in the eyes…small, beady, and black with a new moon sliver of silver when you turn sideways.*

LEO RISING *It's all in the eyes…large, lucent, amber, and ringed with kohl, glittering with the bounce back from cameras flashing.*

VIRGO RISING *It's all in the eyes…breed-standard wolf yellow, with magnifying lenses to see each grain of dirt.*

LIBRA RISING *It's all in the eyes…covered in a midnight silk eye mask as constant moonlight gives you a migraine.*

SCORPIO RISING *It's all in the eyes…black holes, covered by menacing black shades, in case you accidentally see yourself.*

SAGITTARIUS RISING *It's all in the eyes… one red, one black because you dropped a contact lens during your last transformation.*

CAPRICORN RISING *It's all in the eyes… ice blue, with varifocals for efficient power glaring at all distances.*

AQUARIUS RISING *It's all in the eyes…red and green, paw-activated optical units built into your space visor.*

PISCES RISING *It's all in the eyes…watery, but currently behind two eyepatches because your last victim went down fighting.*

Living with your monster

LIVING WITH YOUR MONSTER IS A DAILY CHALLENGE IN EVERY
SCENARIO. HERE ARE THE ANSWERS TO SOME SCORPIO FAQS.

What triggers your monster?

Anything. Nothing. You are in total control at all times, so the Werewolf runs
at your command, a weapon to quell uppity friends if, for example, they want
to go to a grill when you have specified a sushi evening. You also unleash it if
anyone is slavishly obedient (you despise the weak), beats you at anything at
all, or isn't sufficiently frightened of you in normal mode (very rare).
Sometimes, just to show how in control you are, you let the wolf out at
random for no reason.

How does your werewolf do in love?

Even on a good day you are fiercely possessive, jealous, manipulative,
and controlling, as well as the zodiac's sex bomb. This is an unnervingly
popular combo (see *Fifty Shades of Grey*), but has nothing to do with your
Werewolf. That's usually kept on a tight leather leash, but busts out when
your lust slave (a) asks where you have been since last Tuesday, (b) glances
at the shelf where you keep your secret diary, (c) gets mad when you read
their secret diary, (d) mentions someone they knew in high school, or (e)
asks to be untied for an unscheduled comfort break. You savage them into
submission with freezing silences, ominous stillness, and the laser glare. If
you are a Scorpio male, you are the lone wolf our mothers warned us about.
If you are a Scorpio female, you are Angua von Uberwald, the Discworld's
werewolf cop.

What does your werewolf do at work?

Look, you're the sign that wears their inner monster on the outside, if
coworkers lack basic self-preservation skills, they get culled—nature's
way. You are either the boss, self-employed, or on skid row. As boss, you

have no regrets about the monthly bloodbath that is the Sales & Progress Meeting, and use the dormant wolf as an efficient and low cost way to crack the whip. As a freelancer, you let the wolf out to scourge yourself on a monthly basis, with surprisingly uplifting results. When you are indulging your degradation habit on the street, the wolf keeps your patch of gutter clear while you look at the stars. And if you have failed yourself and got stuck in a McJob, the Werewolf's yellow glare makes sure line managers are reluctant to sack you, unless you want them to.

How can you tame your monster?

How do you stop your Werewolf from causing havoc? You don't. I can think of no circumstances under which you would want to declaw this fine asset. You already control it, it's not like the tail wags the Werewolf, and you're comfortable with partial nudity, shredded clothes, and the iron scent of drying blood. But hypothetically speaking (I'm thinking out of the box here—don't look at me like that) if you had to, it would be easy. You'd do it all with pure willpower. You'd put yourself in a cake-induced trance, then lock the Werewolf in a metallic room deep inside your soul, and only you would see it again.

GETTING PROTECTION

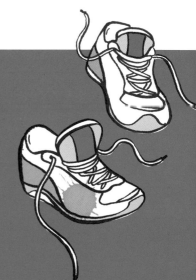

What can the rest of us do to protect ourselves from your implacable Werewolf? Nada. We must accept our fate, and offer ourselves to you like acolytes to a particularly exacting guru. (See, you've done nothing, yet we hand over our power willingly.) Silver bullets? If we got near enough to shoot, one look from you and nerveless digits would drop the gun. Vampire venom? You eat vampires for afternoon tea. Another Scorpio might take you on, but it would be a very long fight to the death. Even keeping an eye on the calendar is no use, as you manifest when you will. The only option is to run away, or surrender to the agonizing, bowel-melting ecstasy of being savaged by you and becoming mini-werewolves ourselves.

SAGITTARIUS

Sagittarius the Archer • November 23–December 21
• Mutable Fire Sign • Positive Sign • Ruled by: Jupiter

You Jekyll...

*The Jekyll is strong in you, Sagittarius, the poster boy for the
glass-not-only-half-full-but-just-the-first-of-many tendency.
Who could feel uncheered after a canter around the park, a
few beers, and a night on the slots with you? Sure, you break
a few hearts, laws, legs, and priceless Ming vases along the way,
but what a Tigger-class ride you are.*

*You are the ninth sign of the zodiac. Nine! Magic Number!
Woah dudes! That's what you call a gang—you and Frodo
and the rest of the guys sticking it to the Eye, saving the
world and stuff. Ruled by the unpredictable element of Fire
and the system's jolliest planet Jupiter, you are the Life and
Soul of the zodiac party.*

...you Hyde

But who has not wilted within at the sight of a
hellbent funtrooper coming our way at full gallop with
a bucket of Horse's Neck, a fistful of Class A substances,
and an endless fund of tactless one liners and insisting
that we go play Blind Man's Base Jump with them.
You're relentless when Hyde is about: rude, crude,
thoughtless, tactless, anarchic minus the cultural theory,
oafish, obnoxious, reckless, irresponsible, mad, bad, and
dangerous to know, but without the Byronic charm.
Red lights signal "go" to you, you'll binge and bet on
anything, and you justify it all by screaming "YOLO"
at us as you skateboard nude the wrong way down the
San Diego Freeway. Pass the trank gun.

Sagittarius: the Racing Demon

You are a Mutable Fire sign. Mutable signs throb like racing cars on the grid, scattering restless energy that gleefully undoes everything Fixed signs got together before grown-up Cardinal signs come along to reestablish order. Fire is the element of action, positivity, desire, destruction, and burning things to the ground. Put 'em together and what have you got? On a calm day, fearless, unquenchable curiosity that fires beams of illumination into the corners of the mind and leads to stuff like the invention of the light bulb, splitting of the atom, chaos theory, etc.; when the wind howls, careless meddling sparks uncontrollable bush fires, inexplicable conflagrations, and blows the lid off Pandora's box.

Do you move so fast that the air around you catches fire from sheer friction? Are you always the one caught with a smoking gun or smoldering match, metaphorically or actually? Demon. I'm guessing you got into bad company in high school, accidentally fell into demontude while wire walking over the hellmouth for a dare, and never really grew out of it. As there's so much mayhem to cause, and so little time, you don't waste any of it in elaborate costume changes, but go for Racing Demon, flickering on and off like wildfire, leaving nothing but a scorch-mark rainbow in the air.

As you survey the damage, are you ambushed by remorse for what calamities you have unleashed? For about 0.005 of a nanosecond, until you perk up, reflame, and point out that it was top-level demoning by you, and no one died. When informed that yes, they did, you slow down to a canter out of respect, then point out that they had a great time and went out with a blast. Tact: not a concept in your quiver.

So how do you manifest?

It's hard to tell. You don't look any different, just hotter, sweatier, and a little bit like Nicholas Cage in *Ghost Rider*. You don't actually get bigger but the world shrinks around you as you fill all available space with heat and hooves, and short out the Risk Perception Network in our brains. You never stand still long enough to be summoned, and just rock up at any devilish crossroads where there is a choice between being sensible (yawn) and doing something dumb that will lead to certain death to play Devil's Advocate. You're the demon who drives us to drink and got us that DUI; you're the demon who slaloms through our minds whispering that we should man up and take Dead Man's Curve at 100mph, bet the college fund on a three-legged horse, go for that "eat a whole steer, and get one free deal." Plus you got arrows, so you don't even have to be on site to cause mayhem—you fire at random, like a badass Cupid, and somewhere in another state there's a prison breakout and spontaneous nude flashmobbing.

[For other demons in the zodiac see Aries and Leo]

Other Evil Influences

A BAND OF DEMON BROTHERS PARTYING IS JUST YOUR CUP OF BRIMSTONE, SO YOU'RE PLEASED TO KNOW THAT YOU'RE NOT ALONE; HOW YOU EXPRESS YOUR DEMONIC DASH IS INFLUENCED BY OTHER ZODIACAL HAPPENINGS; YOUR RULING PLANET, WHERE YOUR MOON IS LURKING, AND WHAT SIGN WAS OOZING OVER THE EASTERN HORIZON AT THE TIME OF YOUR BIRTH.

Bad moon

Your Moon expresses the Inner You. Did you know you had an Inner You? It's a tiny little thing tucked deep inside the universe that is the Outer You, like a fly in a cathedral, but you can hear it buzzing occasionally. Your Moon can be placed in any of the zodiac houses when you are born and modify your monster (although not in a good way, of course). Here's how it affects the Sagittarius Demon.

MOON IN ARIES *Racing Demon with extra demon thrust and no brakes. Unstoppable.*

MOON IN TAURUS *Racing Demon who sticks to the speed limit and builds in plenty of snack breaks.*

MOON IN GEMINI *Racing Demon who can pilot a Lockheed SR-71 Blackbird with one claw and a Bugatti with the other.*

MOON IN CANCER *Racing Demon who lets others win and then gets mad at them.*

MOON IN LEO *Racing Demon who stunt drives in Die Hard movies; and you thought it was all CGI.*

MOON IN VIRGO *Racing Demon who has gone brightside and now works for the local police Rapid Response Unit.*

MOON IN LIBRA *Racing Demon who likes the bit at the end of the race best, with the champagne and adulation.*

MOON IN SCORPIO *Racing Demon who plays chicken run using wolf-drawn sleds; loser gets eaten.*

MOON IN SAGITTARIUS *Racing Demon who has lapped himself and is now temporally confused.*

MOON IN CAPRICORN *Racing Demon behind the holding company that owns the syndicate that owns the racing cars that Sagittarius Rising drives.*

MOON IN AQUARIUS *Racing Demon who drives a retro-fitted steampunk ipsomobile with a Saturn V rocket under the hood.*

MOON IN PISCES *Racing Demon who runs out of gas at the first bend, blames everyone else, and falls asleep at the wheel.*

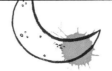

How does your planet bring out your demon?

Provides inexhaustible power to your pitchfork, and the relentless joviality that makes you one of the scarier hellspawn. Sagittarius is ruled by Jupiter, a gas giant so huge and bright it casts shadows on Earth, which whizzes around so fast on its axis that it looks like a Satsuma. It's named for Jupiter, the Roman equivalent of Zeus, team captain of Olympus, who was never at home ruling but always out and about getting into trouble, or causing it.

What's that coming over the hill?

The sign rising over the eastern horizon when you were spawned represents your public persona, your outer appearance; in this case, what kind of Demon you might look like when possessed, or how you would secretly like to manifest in the real world if only you could.

ARIES RISING *Ten feet tall, sweaty, red eyes, possesses reconditioned engines, humvees, fire trucks, demolition derby wrecks, and oil rigs.*

TAURUS RISING *Ten feet tall, sweaty, red eyes, possesses luxury yachts and expensive gym equipment you don't use.*

GEMINI RISING *Ten feet tall, sweaty, four red eyes, possesses roulette wheels, blackjack tables, and all the slots in Vegas.*

CANCER RISING *Ten feet tall, sweaty, red eyes, possesses the family car, 4WD baby strollers, and shopping carts.*

LEO RISING *Ten feet tall, sweaty, red eyes, possesses stage coaches, royal carriages, thoroughbreds, and the presidential motorcade.*

VIRGO RISING *Ten feet tall, sweaty, red eyes, possesses racing bikes, crosstrainers, running machines, and jogging pants.*

LIBRA RISING *Ten feet tall, sweaty, red eyes, possesses luxury limousines, taxis, rickshaws, and the horse-drawn carriages in Central Park.*

SCORPIO RISING *Ten feet tall, sweaty, red eyes, possesses cars with blacked-out windows, Russian roulette guns, and autoerotic bondage kit.*

SAGITTARIUS RISING *Twenty feet tall, extra sweaty, red eyes, possesses bungee lines, poker tables, rodeos, fugu fish, and the school bus.*

CAPRICORN RISING *Ten feet tall, sweaty, red eyes, possesses public utility vehicles, commuter trains, the subway, and all Stock Exchanges.*

AQUARIUS RISING *Ten feet tall, sweaty, red eyes, possesses space modules, rocket boosters, supersonic aircraft, and the Hogwarts Express.*

PISCES RISING *Ten feet tall, sweaty, red eyes, possesses secondhard cars, jet skis, parakites, and all drinking games.*

Living with your monster

LIVING WITH YOUR MONSTER IS A DAILY CHALLENGE IN EVERY
SCENARIO. HERE ARE THE ANSWERS TO SOME SAGITTARIUS FAQs.

What triggers your monster?

You're the zodiac's trigger-happy gunslinger, the demon without a cause,
so the merest hintiest hint of anything tedious can pluck your string: being
held up at a stoplight, a line of more than you at the checkout, big red
buttons that say Do Not Press, any motor vehicle left unattended, especially
if it is a fire truck. If there is no obvious trigger, you'll create one; you are
a ninth level Lord of Misrule and you can kick butt when you want (and
anyway Sagittarius rules the butt and thighs.)

How does your demon do in love?

Technically you're a Demon Lover (demonic frenzy, awesome stamina)
but you can't keep a straight face or do the whole smoldering-eyed
staring thing and silence. You are not the go-to sign for romance and
commitment, so you're rarely around long enough to get demonic on
anyone's ass, but you will go a bit cloven-hoofed if there is any sign of (a)
nagging, (b) mention of quality time together just the two of you, or (c)
demanding to know your real name. You burst into flames (figuratively,
although sometimes literally if it's a hot night), trample the nagger's heart
a bit, set fire to the drapes, and gallop off into the black night. If you are a
Sagittarius male, you are on the tour bus avoiding paternity suits; if you
are a Sagittarius female, you are a runaway bride.

What does your demon do at work?

Disrupt and destabilize. If you're a cowpoke, Texas ranger, or stunt artist,
your demon may never come out, as any demontude will be dissipated
harmlessly on the wind. Statistically you are more likely to be in an office,

but you're not a natural inhabitant of cubicle land. Merely being there gets you in full-on demon mode most of the time. Tethered to an office chair, you tap your hooves constantly, flaring off demonic energy before you start a round of Trashcan Inferno, jam the elevators with the administrator's laptop, plop a brace of clownfish into the water cooler tank, cover yourself in post-its and go to the production meeting as the Office Armadillo, set off the sprinkler system to get the afternoon off, and swap the lids of everyone's coffee. Hilair. They fire you, but not before you quit.

How can you tame your monster?

Whassat? You love your Demon. It gives you an adrenaline edge. If you got it to lie in its basket, you would be dull, diminished, unbounced. If it were a condition of parole, you'd scour Wikipedia for a magic potion guaranteed either to work OR kill you (60:40, great odds) or a sacred ritual involving dangling over a sulfur-filled abyss for nine hours. Way more dangerous than just demoning. In the slammer, you could slot in some hours in the prison library, watch *Buffy* reruns, then when they let you out, you could be a competitive Demon Hunter. You won't feel like a traitor: you're a centaur, and no one knows what side they're on.

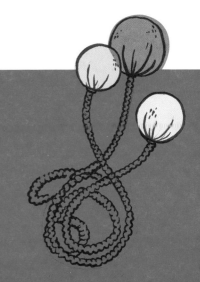

GETTING PROTECTION

What can the rest of us do to protect ourselves from your demonic ridiculous stunts? Technically you can be repelled by holy water, salt, iron, and pentacles, but what are the odds? You can't resist any chance to crash and burn, so bring it on; the holy water would be down your throat in one, your junk food habit shows how much you don't care about sodium levels, amulets are for wimps, and iron horseshoes just make it easier to kick your way out of a pentangle. Best to shore up our own defenses, buy more insurance, and devise a self-protecting mantra to recite when you dare us to do something rash. Thinking laterally, you are allergic to order, so a well-thrown bolas of red tape might bring you down, or at least hobble you....

CAPRiCORN

Capricorn the Goat • December 22–January 20
• Cardinal Earth Sign • Negative Sign • Ruled by: Saturn

You Jekyll...

It's not a barrel of laughs being the zodiac's Designated Adult, is it Capricorn? But you shoulder the burden because you are hardy and hardworking. You have to be, being born at the bottom of the year when the only way is up. Life is a very serious business, as you remind us quite often. You are the ant, sensei—we are but grasshoppers.

You are the tenth sign of the zodiac (that's ten, the basis of counting and order in the western world), ruled by Earth, the only element you can hold fast in a tight fist, and ruled by Saturn, the planet that was once known as The Great Limiter because it patrolled the known rim of the solar system.

...you Hyde

Limiting is your thing, no? Putting an end to unproductive fun; smothering any flickers of spontaneity before they actualize; elevating frugality to an art form. Putting the family on two meals a day not because they are rotund, but because it brings your weekly grocery spend down to single figures. Turning the thermostat down a notch every day. Switching off peripheral vision and focusing all thought and action on one thing: climbing the ladder. You are Parsimonious Tightwad, from Dickens's lost short story of the same name. Surely you don't have the time or the mindset to develop an inner monster…but I see you've got two for the price of one. Excellent value.

Capricorn: Vlad ~~the Impaler~~

You are a Cardinal Earth Sign. Cardinal signs are the CEOs of Zodiac Holdings, establishing the ground rules. Earth is solid, in a real estate and landlocked small empire kind of way, and generates the kerching of hard cash. When your economy is bullish you are the realizer of dreams and the builder of castles on the ground rather than in the air; when it's tanking, the walls close in around you and the earth that guarantees your immortality falls grain by grain through a sinkhole in the fabric of the universe, melting away like a busted Ponzi scheme.

So: earth, narrow focus, control, possession, ability to suck souls dry while leaving blood and bone intact, keen on impaling your workforce to their desks and burying them in paperwork? Your monster is…Scrooge! No, Vampire (although it hasn't been proved that Ebenezer wasn't Undead). As an assiduous social climber, you go to the top, man, Vlad the Impaler. What about your second monster? Well, that belongs to your Goat; your miserly miser rep is so full-screen that it's easy to miss those little goat's hooves twinkling under your pinstripes; half banker, half goat, all satyr. That's what lends your workaholic Vampire its sexual bat squeak and lures people in.

After a hard day sucking the marrow out other people's lives and not even using it, do you feel you've been a shade too cruel? No. It's an effective management tool, and there are plenty of willing fools. You are, however, very ashamed of your Goat and deny absolutely everything when it gets out after you have been drinking with a client at their expense. Writs fly if anyone mentions that night you were out pole dancing with the demons, covered in glitter honey, in a Tokyo karaoke lounge.

So how do you manifest?

Constantly. So you would have us believe, to keep us on the outside edge of our comfort zone even when you know the Vampire is tucked up in its casket. When you are coming on the full Vlad, people can feel you three blocks away just like Renfield, Dracula's wretch, who knew when the master was coming by the patterns the flies made. Life loses any gloss and we sag into megagloom like Marvin the Paranoid Android trapped in 13-episode Scandi noir with a couple of Dementors. Light dims (but that could be because you have fitted low-wattage energy-saving bulbs that only come on when everyone's left) and the air chills (but then you always turn the heating off). You look much the same, but your eyes go a bit oblong (thank your Goat for that) and then all we remember is glazing into unconsciousness as the will to live drains away. It's easier to spot when your Goat is going satyr, as you kick up your heels, bound onto a table, down a magnum of Franzia, and proposition the entire accounts department.

[For other vampires in the zodiac see Taurus and Virgo]

Other Evil Influences

YOU ONLY ACCEPT INPUT FROM VERIFIABLE SOURCES, SO IGNORE QUITE
A LOT OF THIS; NEVERTHELESS, HOW YOU EXPRESS YOUR VAMPIRE STYLE IS
INFLUENCED BY OTHER ZODIACAL HAPPENINGS; YOUR RULING PLANET, WHERE
YOUR MOON IS LURKING, AND WHAT SIGN WAS OOZING OVER THE EASTERN
HORIZON AT THE TIME OF YOUR BIRTH.

Bad moon

Your Moon expresses the Inner You. As Outer You applies top-level privacy settings
on all social media, and the Moon has not been licensed to express anything about
you, you would prefer we didn't read this. Injunctions have been issued. Your Moon
can be placed in any of the zodiac houses when you are born and modify your monster
(although not in a good way, of course). Here's how it affects the Capricorn Vampire.

MOON IN ARIES *The Impaler who impales because it makes you feel just awesome.*

MOON IN TAURUS *The Impaler who impales to extend and maintain the empire; your spike is made to order by Leatherman.*

MOON IN GEMINI *The Impaler who impales with very sharp fine wits.*

MOON IN CANCER *The Impaler who doesn't like impaling but will spike anyone who disrespects the family.*

MOON IN LEO *The Impaler who impales because it's your Destiny; you are Vlad Tepes, are you not, Voivode of Wallachia? Well then.*

MOON IN VIRGO *The Impaler who regretfully only impales friends and enemies when they refuse to do things the right way (yours).*

MOON IN LIBRA *The Impaler who impales to cull the poor and ugly and restore balance to the world.*

MOON IN SCORPIO *The Impaler who impales with a poisoned spike, several times, just to make sure.*

MOON IN SAGITTARIUS *The Impaler who impales a bit, then uses the spike as a crampon for free-climbing jaunts in the Carpathians.*

MOON IN CAPRICORN *The Impaler who impales other impalers.*

MOON IN AQUARIUS *The Impaler who spurns the spike and uses a light saber instead.*

MOON IN PISCES *The Impaler who impales self accidentally after a misunderstanding at a cheese- and blood-tasting evening.*

How does your planet bring out your vampire?

It's got the rings of authority, so it makes your victims lose the will to live. Capricorn is ruled by Saturn, once the solar system's border patrol, but now working indoors in an administrative capacity. It's named for Saturn, the jolly Roman god of agriculture who liked a good time on Saturday night, but who sold out to the Greek conglomerate Cronos. Inc., and is now the curmudgeon of the zodiac.

What's that coming over the hill?

The sign rising over the eastern horizon when you were spawned represents your public persona, your outer appearance; in this case, what kind of Vampire you might look like when possessed, or how you would secretly like to manifest in the real world if only you could.

ARIES RISING *Action Vlad. Full stakeproof armor, Kevlar cape, Teflon fangs with enhanced blood channels, telescopic Impaling Device (pike).*

TAURUS RISING *Connoisseur Vlad. Burgundy silk quilted dressing gown, casket lined with fine calf's leather, cellarful of vintage Bull's Blood.*

GEMINI RISING *Fun Vlad. Yes really. The Twins let the Goat out: skinny jeans, tattoos, queen of the Castle's all-night Silent Disco.*

CANCER RISING *Dress down Vlad. Homemade tux, homespun cape, thrift store fangs, the easy way to mingle with the peasantry.*

LEO RISING *Royal Vlad. Full-on claret velvet dress robes, cape of office, formal fangs, gold-embossed ceremonial impaling spike.*

VIRGO RISING *Dust-mote Vlad. It's much easier to spy on your subjects when you are a cloud of tiny particles.*

LIBRA RISING *Diplomat Vlad. Impeccable tailoring, groomed eyebrows, capped fangs, impaling spike secreted inside ebony walking cane.*

SCORPIO RISING *Rock God Vlad. Black leather pants, black leather cape, diamond in one fang, impales with icy stare; shouldn't work, but it does.*

SAGITTARIUS RISING *Out-of-Office Vlad. All-weather neoprene tux, cape that doubles as a tent, unflossed fangs, impales from distance with arrows.*

CAPRICORN RISING *Business Vlad. Charcoal business suit and matching cape, retractable titanium fangs, impaling spike hidden in unbreakable contract.*

AQUARIUS RISING *Replicant Vlad: undetectable V-class android in traditional tux and cape, takes over while you are in the lab.*

PISCES RISING *Morning After Vlad. Crumpled tux, shredded cape, one broken fang, bent spike, and not in your own casket.*

 Living with your monster

LIVING WITH YOUR MONSTER IS A DAILY CHALLENGE IN EVERY SCENARIO. HERE ARE THE ANSWERS TO SOME CAPRICORN FAQS.

What triggers your monster?

Lights left on. Disrespect for your status; excess fun; any fun; grasshoppers (see page 83); practical jokes; not being taken seriously; being denied your pound of flesh. Once triggered, your Vampire is relentless; anyone who gives you the run around faces endless litigation and an almighty bill for compensation. You have all the time in eternity, remorseless stamina thanks to Saturn, and a hotline to Hades via the Goat, and we all know how hot the Prince of Darkness is on contractual obligation.

How does your vampire do in love?

Love is wasteful and irrational. You are looking for a profitable merger of assets and property, cemented by a solid contract with cast-iron clauses, so you shouldn't have to go Bat; but the Vampire will come out and suck any romance from the scene when (a) other people are invited for an extravagant two–course meal on your birthday, (b) lovers complain because you won't say the L-word, (c) they want to actually wear the platinum studs you invested in, (d) they get promoted a rung higher than you. That you have any lovers at all is down to your Goat, which lends an erotic allure to your immaculate portfolio. If you are a Capricorn male, women hope you might be Mr. Darcy; if you are a Capricorn female, you know that diamonds are a girl's best friend.

What does your vampire do at work?

Industrious goats do not stop nibbling and climbing all day, and neither do you. Work is your natural habitat and it's where your Vampire feels most at home, ensuring budgets are cut to the bone (Capricorn rules the bones).

You suffer from chronic presenteeism, and believe that all work and no play makes Vlad a rich and respected pillar of Undead society. The Vampire rises when (a) somebody who isn't last night's cleaning crew running late gets in before you, (b) your name is not on the door, even though there isn't a door, (c) it's Dressed-Down Friday, (d) the style and quality of your office chair does not match your rank and position, (e) your parking space is reallocated. Your Satyr only shows up at Office Party season.

How can you tame your monster?

That box is already ticked. You've scrunched the numbers and know how effective your Vampire is at controlling hearts and minds. It would be economic insanity not to keep it on the payroll. However, there have been too many workforce suicides lately (you have no legal responsibility; they read the contract) and you're getting damaging press which may impact on your upward mobility, so perhaps it would be politic to keep Vlad in his casket. Method: (1) Download ancestry.app and distract your Vampire by working out how Vlad is related to the crowned heads of Europe. Method: (2) invest in a sunlamp and make yourself sunbathe three times a day.

GETTING PROTECTION

What can the rest of us do to protect ourselves from being swamped by the existential lassitude and tristesse-de-vivre after a Vlad attack? Will traditional remedies work, as you are very traditional? Crucifix? Your Goat's demonic connections neutralizes that one. Stake? Your heart may be too tiny to be a viable target. Garlic? You don't eat foreign food. We could band together and build an impenetrable wall of cheerfulness, which will involve lots of whistling, smiling, and looking on the bright side and will be very tiring. Maybe encourage the Goat, ply you with liquor and let it and the Vampire duke it out? For everyday help, we should habitually carry Tootsie Rolls and/or a Krispy Kreme donut for an instant serotonin fix after an attack.

AQUARIUS

Aquarius the Water Carrier • January 21–February 19
• Fixed Air Sign • Positive Sign
• Ruled by: Uranus (and Saturn, a bit)

You Jekyll...

OK you are willfully left field, obstinately whacky, and maybe your choice of leg wear is a bit random, but your heart is in the right place, approximately, and while there are whales to be saved, ecosystems to be defended, and human rights to be fought for, you are out there on Team Angel, although your mom might wish you called home a bit more often.

You are the eleventh sign of the zodiac. Eleven is a Master Number (thanks Numerology guys) marking you out as a Seeker on Another Path. Cool huh? Didn't you always know you were Different? Ruled by the element Air and Uranus, the system's most oddball planet. Saturn, your old ruler, just didn't "get" you: you are a free spirit.

...you Hyde

That should be a clue, I suppose. You're already a spirit, but are you the good or bad kind? (It's a smart move, means you can get away with being chilly, distant, disengaged, rude, obstinate, too cool for your own T-shirt, and always ready to experiment with other people's feelings because you don't seem to have any of your own.) The trail of puzzlement and heartbreak you leave behind is written off as collateral damage, interesting but unimportant, and nothing to do with you. But maybe *La Condition Humaine* is an uncomfortable fit for you because you don't understand it; maybe you ain't even from these parts, partner. Maybe you ain't from this galaxy. Where does it say you can't be an alien with an Inner Monster?

Aquarius: The Ghost in the Machine

You are a Fixed Air sign. Just because you are called the Water Carrier, everyone thinks that you are a water sign. That would be far too ordinary; the water that pours from your pitcher is a metaphor for free-flowing mental energy, all right? Fixed signs keep things in focus and do not let themselves be sidetracked by emotion. (Laser lights, not disco ball.) And Air is the element of thought and intellect. When you're in good spirits, data, concepts, and intuition fuse together and suddenly the elegant helical structure of DNA, say, reveals itself. When you're in bad spirits, knowledge goes Darkside, and suddenly you're thinking that Mutally Assured Destruction is a good thing.

Chilliness, the two second delay in your response, as if you are beaming in from another dimension, odd clothes that look they could be from a different era, and probably are, inability to physically engage: it all adds up to Ghost. You don't correct us; our little earthcentric brains could not take it. Back on your home planet just off Tau Ceti you're an ordinary B-class *cbrxyblz Vm*, but here on Earth you are something special. No one knows what you really look like. A pillar of silicon? A cloud of methane? A small bipedal mushroom? Only earthling cats see you for what you are, and they won't tell us.

Is it not against the Federation's directive to interfere with other life-forms by scaring them witless? Have you no concern for the Butterfly Effect? No, because (1) guilt, remorse, and shame are emotions to which you have no access and (2) there are too few Aquarians on Earth to make any statistically meaningful impact. You're never going to get caught because your technology is way too advanced. Mulder & Scully came close, but that was years ago.

So how do you manifest?

Unnervingly, and never when expected. You look your usual slightly off beam self, maybe a bit more insubstantial, and it gets colder around you, but mostly it's the sensation of impossible movements just outside our peripheral vision. You seem to flicker on and off, and appear suddenly in places where you couldn't possibly be. "Ghost!" scream our collective goose bumps, rising to the occasion, as this is what Ghosts do. Actually it's because the transporter beam you use to project your hologrammatic avatar gets a little glitchy when the solar wind blows up, or you are pissed. Well, it is 12 light years away, already 3 OSs out of date, and needs a serious upgrade. What's really scary is the backlash we get when you are disrespected on your home planet (someone's used your special Xuuul!tk maybe), triggering your Real Inner Monster, and you accidentally (on purpose) beam down a strobing image of a writhing tentacled thing with reversed-out guts, 67 eyes, and parts of itself in the eighth dimension; this is what really gives us the heebie-jeebies. And you don't have to do anything.

[For other ghosts in the zodiac see Gemini and Libra]

Other Evil Influences

THE MORE INPUT THE BETTER; IT ALL HELPS TO CREATE A DATABASE OF AVATARS FOR YOU TO CHOOSE FROM. HOW YOU EXPRESS YOUR SPECTRAL STYLE IS INFLUENCED BY OTHER ZODIACAL HAPPENINGS; YOUR RULING PLANET, WHERE YOUR MOON IS LURKING, AND WHAT SIGN WAS OOZING OVER THE EASTERN HORIZON AT THE TIME OF YOUR BIRTH.

Bad moon

Your Moon expresses the Inner You. There is no Earthling terminology to explain the real Inner You, but you're happy to go along with whatever human astrology has to offer in the way of modifications to the basic model. Your Moon can be placed in any of the zodiac houses when you are born and modify your monster (although not in a good way, of course). Here's how it affects the Aquarius Ghost.

MOON IN ARIES *Earthlings are passive and lack the killer instinct. They'd be instantly chopped liver back home on Mars.*

MOON IN TAURUS *How you miss the slow twirl of Venus. A creamy dawn, then 243 tiny Earthling days until bedtime. Luxury.*

MOON IN GEMINI *On Mercury, you were a slow hand; here you are quick-draw.*

MOON IN CANCER *It's kind of comforting to see home from here, but you wish mom would stop sending souvenir moonrock.*

MOON IN LEO *Earthlings don't believe you are from the heart of the Sun.*

MOON IN VIRGO *Earth is slow, grimy, and inefficiently run; you pine for the fast, sleek shininess of your home planet Mercury.*

MOON IN LIBRA *Since landing, your skin has turned to sandpaper and your hair is unmanageable; oh for some Venusian cloud cover.*

MOON IN SCORPIO *Disney-based jokes about your planet's name are not appreciated.*

MOON IN SAGITTARIUS *Hey Earthling Dudes, lost your fun buttons? Come back to my place (Jupiter), we can surf some rings.*

MOON IN CAPRICORN *Saturnian colleagues will be shocked when you report the number of earth hours wasted on nonreproductive sex.*

MOON IN AQUARIUS *You've logged all the anatomical puns now, and can't wait to get back to Uranus for some adult conversation.*

MOON IN PISCES *Neptune's cold, wet, and far away; let's stay in the bar.*

How does your planet bring out your ghost?

Imparts an unearthly coldness—it has no inner heat source; and explains the oddball—it spins on its side. After far too long, yoked with megadull Capricorn under Saturn's thumb, Aquarius is now ruled by Uranus, a modern planet in Earth terms, discovered in 1781 when the United Federation sent William Herschel the coordinates. It's named for Ouranos, the suitably distant Greek god of the Sky.

What's that coming over the hill?

The sign rising over the eastern horizon when you were spawned represents your public persona, your outer appearance; in this case, what kind of Ghost you might look like when possessed, or how you would secretly like to manifest in the real world if only you could.

ARIES RISING *The Ghost in the chainsaw that makes it slip, severing the town's electricity cable and the user's own leg.*

TAURUS RISING *The Ghost in the bank Vault that transports gold bars and banker's drafts to Switzerland without the IRS noticing.*

GEMINI RISING *The Ghost in the OS system that crashes our whole digital world across all delivery platforms for no reason.*

CANCER RISING *The Ghost in the kitchen that switches the freezer off and makes sure that the cooker timer never works.*

LEO RISING *The Ghost in the lighting rig that mis-cues entire performance and keeps the spots upstage when we are down.*

VIRGO RISING *The Ghost in the database that ensures all data is mismatched, passwords are invalid, and our credit ratings tank.*

LIBRA RISING *The Ghost in the beauty parlor that tans us orange and frizzes our hair.*

SCORPIO RISING *The Ghost of any control system whose failure will result in death carnage, mayhem, eternal grief, and endless lawsuits.*

SAGITTARIUS RISING *The Ghost in the altimeter that takes our paraglider so high we're freeze-dried, or so low we smack into Brooklyn Bridge.*

CAPRICORN RISING *The Ghost in the White House that has run everything since 1969; so far no one has busted you.*

AQUARIUS RISING *The Ghost in the Internet, spying on us all and selling the information to Offworld Marketing Syndicates.*

PISCES RISING *The Ghost in the Sat Nav that gets us lost, which is why we're three days late for own wedding.*

Living with your monster

LIVING WITH YOUR MONSTER IS A DAILY CHALLENGE IN EVERY
SCENARIO. HERE ARE THE ANSWERS TO SOME AQUARIUS FAQS.

What triggers your monster?

It's hard to predict (that's the way you like it), as it could be something
that happened on your home planet. Here on Earth, you can come over all
Ghost (unnervingly silent, cold, stand offish, and that whole simultaneously
impenetrable yet insubstantial thing) when (a) you're forced into a one-to-
one meeting, (b) interrupted in whatever you're doing for what someone
else wants to do, and (c) you feel like it.

How does your ghost do in love?

Love (whatever that is) only works for you if the Other lives on another
continent, is way out of your league in either direction, or related to a mortal
enemy (Montague/Capulet, Shark/Jet) so you only meet up every Transit of
Venus and the likelihood of icky-sticky togetherness is remote. You are just
not that into them. Or anybody. When you say you "need space" you mean it,
as you can't achieve lift off and return to orbit in the confines of a relationship.
The Ghost's mission is to freeze off any intimacy—with surly looks, nil body
contact, snarky one-line putdowns—when threatened by, say (a) a date with
just the two of you, (b) your laptop switching off during sex, and (c) a couple's
massage. If you are an Aquarius male, women persist on trying to unfreeze
your heart. If you are an Aquarius female, lovesick bards write sonnets about
your faraway icy beauty; very tedious.

What does your ghost do at work?

You'll do anything—street sweeper, derivatives shark, test pilot—that
doesn't involve hierarchies or professional caring, but your natural home
is IT. As you are already an alien consciousness interfacing with an

unfamiliar piece of carbon-based kit, it's only a click way from being the resident Ghost in the machinery that runs all workplaces. Your Ghost doesn't need a trigger; it's constantly on shift, modeling what-if scenarios for research purposes. (What if…all the NASDAQ software went down simultaneously?) Screens freeze, the system chokes on spam, the CEO is trapped in the safe by the automatic timing system going rogue? You can bring a megacorps to its corporate knees in half a day, and you don't even have to be there to do it. Absenteeism is one of your core skills.

How can you tame your monster?

Does not compute. What monster? Maybe Operation Human doesn't run as smoothly as projected, but that's what makes it exciting for a cosmic anthropologist like you. It isn't your fault that humans misread your avatar, and that their cultural mindsets cast you as a Ghost. But it's true that many of your laboratory rats get injured during experiments, and you don't want damaged samples, so perhaps you should have a redesign. Try modifying the software: reconfigure the empathy drive, and upgrade the Intimacy plug-in, or at least improve the fuel flow (Aquarius rules the circulation) in the heating unit.

GETTING PROTECTION

What can the rest of us do to protect ourselves from your heart chilling otherworldly presence? Whatever we do, you just laugh in a cold, cardonic Dr Peter Venkman manner at our quaint ineffective folk remedies. As you permeate our skin with hopeless dread (a by-product of the experiment), maybe some form of emotional fat-suit would work, a notional covering made out of happy thoughts and red velvet cupcakes? Or, as you are a virtual entity anyway, we could just visualize your molecules shut up in a cramped, hot container, like Aladdin's lamp. (He should never have let you out.) Or, best, we could just not engage with you, refuse to take part in the experiment, and ruin your research program so your funding is withdrawn.

PISCES

Pisces the Fish • February 20th–March 20th
• Mutable Water Sign • Negative Energy
• Ruled by: Neptune (and Jupiter, a bit)

You Jekyll...

If the zodiac were a (rather overpopulated) boy band, you, Pisces, would be The Sensitive One. Dreamy, romantic, sentimental, a bit of a softie, you feel the pull of everyone else's emotional tides, plumbing our pain and joy, often more deeply than we do ourselves, which can occasionally feel a little intrusive; some depths are best left murky, don't you think?

You are the twelfth sign, the end of the rainbow, or the end of the line, depending on which of your fish is swimming the strongest at the time. You are ruled by the element water and the planet Neptune, named for the god of the sea and altered states. All the zodiacal overflow pours into you, and it does slop over every now and again.

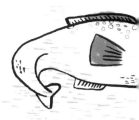

...you Hyde

At least that is what you plead when you have got yourself into another fine mess, because personal responsibility is not a core value. Core anything does not float your boat as it implies a backbone, and you only have bendy cartilage, but this is not your fault, as you are a fish. Human kind cannot bear very much reality but you, Pisces, are having none of it. You spend most of the time in a world of your own which is renewed every six hours, scoured clean like a beach, so you can start a lovely new fantasy without the inconvenience of incriminating evidence from the last one. This allows you to believe that you didn't do what you did, or that you did do what you didn't.

Pisces: the Sea Werewolf

You are a Mutable Water sign. Mutable signs are the ones that either destroy everyone else's hard work and mess everything up OR break up tired, oppressive, old systems so that fresh, new oppressive systems can be built. Or both. Change and Chaos, the Pisces' house cocktail. Water is the element of the emotions, powerful, unpredictable, uplifting, destructive, and very difficult to nail to the wall. And you, Pisces, are splashing about in a whole ocean of it. On calm days, you go blamelessly with the flow; when a storm blows in from out of nowhere, the waters churn and boil, and hideous monsters arise from the depths to devour the unwary.

I told you that Pisces contains the rest of the zodiac's used bathwater, right. So identifying your inner monster isn't straightforward. The empathy junkie that sucks on everyone else's emotional scars points to Vampire; the unreliable, unsubstantial fantasist could mean Ghost. Ah, but the whiny self-pity, the brain fog, the flickering mood swings, the I-am-helpless-in-the-claws-of-accursed-fate, the secret joy of tearing other people's emotional guts out all add up to Werewolf. A Sea Werewolf, of course. Although this is just you bigging yourself up, as a Sea Wolf is really a kind of catfish, but why let the facts ruin a perfectly fine fantasy.

Fish are slippery, and when it comes to ducking and diving and planting bloodstained garments on innocent bystanders, you are the master. If caught, you don't admit to your Werewolf and face up to your responsibilities. After denying the evidence of the blood and feathers around your mouth, you hold up your paws/fins whine that you can't remember anything, that the monster takes over and forces you to do unspeakable acts against your will.

So how do you manifest?

Predictably unpredictably. We know that you will go Wolf but not when. You are the sign with the built-in Heisenberg Principle. In the real world, where the rest of us live, you don't change physically, although your eyes may get beadier, and there's a distinct (for once) impression of purpose, as if both your fish have got themselves into alignment. In your world, you imagine yourself to be a yellow-eyed superlupine with unspecified awesome powers. Wolf time can last from a couple of seconds to a few years, or even a lifetime. Your wolf can sniff out anybody's vulnerable underbelly rip it out in an instant, and be off again. The bonus is you can then get your empathy fix from your victim's distress even though you're the one who caused it, like the walrus sobbing over the fate of the oysters. Even better, because you're a Machiavelli-class manipulator, you can play the helpless card, and get all the attention switched to poor little you, while your victim bleeds out, ignored, in the corner.

[For other werewolves in the zodiac see Cancer and Scorpio]

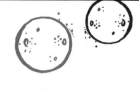

Dark Stars

A WHOLE RAFT OF ALTERNATIVE REALITIES, WITHOUT YOU EVEN HAVING TO DREAM THEM UP? YAY! HOW YOU EXPRESS YOUR WEREWOLF STYLE IS INFLUENCED BY OTHER ZODIACAL HAPPENINGS: YOUR RULING PLANET, WHERE YOUR MOON IS LURKING, AND WHAT SIGN WAS OOZING OVER THE EASTERN HORIZON AT THE TIME OF YOUR BIRTH.

Bad moon

Your Moon expresses the Inner You, or rather your Outer You(s) is/are evasive, slippery, but your Inner Yous (it's like a Hall of Mirrors in there) are surprisingly smart operators and what keep you afloat, rather like a shark's swim bladder. Your Moon can be placed in any of the zodiac houses when you are born and modify your monster (although not in a good way, of course). Here's how it affects the Pisces Werewolf.

MOON IN ARIES *Accidental Werewolf made during the confusion after Operation Red Riding Hood was compromised by civilian woodcutters.*
MOON IN TAURUS *Accidental Werewolf made because you were convinced that the animal was a handsome wealthy prince under a curse.*
MOON IN GEMINI *Accidental twin Werewolves, made during an unwise romance on a skiing vacation in Eastern Europe. Fun though.*
MOON IN CANCER *Accidental Werewolf made by empathizing strongly with Remus Lupin.*
MOON IN LEO *Accidental Werewolf made during the casting session for the* Twilight *trilogy.*
MOON IN VIRGO *Accidental Werewolf made when volunteering at a wolf sanctuary and using your own herbal remedy (wolfsbane) for hard pad.*

MOON IN LIBRA *Accidental Werewolf. You've forgotten how, but stick with it because you can justify a new closet after every transformation.*
MOON IN SCORPIO *Nonaccidental Werewolf, made to find out if you could control it.*
MOON IN SAGITTARIUS *Accidental Werewolf made when you fell off the Iditarod sled and misidentified one of the huskies.*
MOON IN CAPRICORN *Accidental Werewolf made on a work-related trip to Wall Street.*
MOON IN AQUARIUS *Accidental Werewolf made because you thought going for the throat was a harmless earthling greeting ritual.*
MOON IN PISCES *Accidental Werewolf made in a seafront bar on your birthday.*

How does your planet bring out your werewolf?

Blurs the line between reality and fantasy so you can slip in and out easily; it's a huge, hazy ball of bluish fog that lurches slowly sideways around the Sun, pulling a raggle-taggle crew of moons and broken rings after it. Once you were Jupiter's plaything, but it was much too hard-edged, and now you are much happier with Neptune, named for the Roman god of the sea, Jupiter's lost soul of a brother.

What's that coming over the hill?

The sign rising over the eastern horizon when you were spawned represents your public persona, your outer appearance; in this case, what kind of Werewolf you might look like when possessed, or how you would secretly like to manifest in the real world if only you could.

ARIES RISING *In your dreams…a pirate Werewolf with a trident, a brace of cutlasses, and a demonic cackle.*

TAURUS RISING *In your dreams…a matador Werewolf, with extra long fangs and a suit of black lights, like fish scales.*

GEMINI RISING *In your dreams…two devil-may-care highwaymen Werewolves, one for each fish, on coal black mares.*

CANCER RISING *In your dreams…mafiosa Werewolf with shipping connections who can make with linguine al vongole to die for.*

LEO RISING *In your dreams…big game hunter Werewolf in a safari suit mauled by lions and a jeep full of guns.*

VIRGO RISING *In your dreams…an ER surgeon Werewolf in red scrubs, with a neat way of stitching up ripped skin.*

LIBRA RISING *In your dreams…a Trophy Wife Werewolf, with the bad girl yellow eyes that drives rich old billionaires wild with desire.*

SCORPIO RISING *In your dreams…plutocrat Werewolf who secretly controls the world and whose vineyards produce the devil's black wine.*

SAGITTARIUS RISING *In your dreams… wreck-hunting Werewolf who dives without a scuba kit and has a pet shark on a string.*

CAPRICORN RISING *In your dreams… lawyer Werewolf with all the smarts who will get the rest of you off with community service.*

AQUARIUS RISING *In your dreams… robo-Werewolf: part wolf, part fish, part rustproof self-maintaining alien technology.*

PISCES RISING *In your dreams…navy SEAL Werewolf: fit, fast, smart competent, sober, defender of the way of the Wolf.*

Living with your monster

LIVING WITH YOUR MONSTER IS A DAILY CHALLENGE IN EVERY
SCENARIO. HERE ARE THE ANSWERS TO SOME PISCES FAQS.

What triggers your monster?

The unbearable pressure of human existence, being asked to do
something you don't want to do, the bar running out of absinthe, heartless
interrogation by unkind people who want to know where you have
been all week…you are hypersensitive, it's a curse you bear as best you
can. Everything that cruder souls take in their stride lacerates you, reality
dissolves, and you go Werewolf, or so they tell you, but they could be lying.

How does your werewolf do in love?

You are the Romantic sign and can only function when bathed in a
bottomless sea of unconditional love. As this is unrealistic when you are
grown up, your Werewolf is one busy monster, going for the throat when
lovers get all demanding and high maintenance, and ask intrusive questions
such as what is your name. It also comes in handy when you have (a) been
out all night and come home covered in long red hairs, (b) been out all
night and never come home, or (c) get caught out in what we call a lie and
you call an alternative version. The Werewolf does the savaging then you
blame your lover. Look what they made you do. If you're a Pisces male,
you are the pirate gypsy all women's mothers warn them about; if you're a
Pisces female, you are constantly enraged about the number of frogs you've
got to kiss before you get a prince.

What does your werewolf do at work?

You are at work under protest, as in Mittytopia (where you live in
your head) you have an unlimited private income and shoes made of
unobtainium (Pisces rules the feet). Your Werewolf works harder than you,

leaping out of the darkness when (a) accounts questions your expense sheet, (b) HR questions the length of your lunch breaks, and (c) at every progress meeting. Of course you have made no progress; you've been playing Angry Birds all week, but you have no problem blaming everyone else in the team for the loss of the prestigious Warbucks account, as in your capacity as Caring Good Listener you know all their little problems and awkwardnesses and can blackmail them into taking the rap. You can do this on your own, of course, but it's good to have the Werewolf as muscle.

How can you tame your monster?

Well you'd have to admit to it first, and that would mean Taking Responsibility, which is a big step for a zodiac animal that doesn't have legs. Besides, you love your Werewolf; it's an escape from this cruel world, an alternative reality with real bite, and a perfect counterpoint to your wishy-washy bleeding heart public persona. If you had to, like the judge insisted, you'd consent to compulsory therapy. You wouldn't have to pay for it, it's all about you, it gets you out of the office, and if you're smart, will go on forever as you'll never make the therapeutic breakthrough, will you? If you don't get cured, you can blame the shrink.

GETTING PROTECTION

What can the rest of us do to protect ourselves from emotional shredding? Traditionally, we've got holy water and silver bullets. Holy water would be just a drop in your ocean. And have you tried shooting fish if they're not in a barrel? What we must not do is to feel sorry for you (the King Kong effect); we'll drown in the sea of misery created when you slash through the chinks in our emotional armor and let out all the fear and loathing. So, being practical here, maybe a lifebelt? We'd have to all make our own out of Positive Affirmations and Happy Thoughts. As a desperate measure, a well-aimed quart of whiskey will distract the Werewolf while we swim away.

When Monsters Collide

What if your monster were to gang up with other monsters? Who could you work with to cause maximum havoc? Who would ally with you, who would sabotage you, who would cancel out your powers? Consult the chart to find out.

Remember:

- monsters from the same sun sign can either work in perfect, hideous partnership or eclipse each other
- monsters who vibrate at a similar energy level can work together even though they are from different species
- monsters from the same element can form formidable alliances even though their energy levels are different
- monsters from opposite signs★ understand each other, but may be implacable enemies
- demons (Fire) do not ally with werewolves (Water) but will work with vampires (Earth) and ghosts (Air)
- vampires (Earth) do not ally with ghosts (Air) but will work with demons (Fire) and werewolves (Water)★★
- ghosts (Air) do not ally with vampires (Earth) but will work with demons (Fire) and werewolves (Water)
- werewolves (Water) do not ally with demons (Fire) but will work with vampires (Earth) and ghosts (Air)
- demons work best with ghosts, but tolerate vampires
- vampires work best with werewolves, but will tolerate demons
- ghosts work best with demons but will tolerate werewolves
- werewolves work best with vampires but will tolerate ghosts

★ Your opposite sign is the one six signs away, directly opposite you on the zodiac wheel. You have a very strong connection via your energies, but it doesn't show on the surface.

★★ Do not believe the implacable enmity myth—werewolves and vampires are in an eternity-long relationship.

	Aries	Taurus	Gemini	Cancer	Leo	Virgo	Libra	Scorpio	Sagittarius	Capricorn	Aquarius	Pisces
Aries	0	5	6	3	2	5	1	4	2	3	6	4
Taurus	5	0	4	6	3	2	5	1	4	2	3	6
Gemini	6	4	0	5	6	3	2	5	1	4	2	3
Cancer	3	6	5	0	4	6	3	2	4	1	5	2
Leo	2	3	6	4	0	5	6	3	2	5	1	4
Virgo	5	2	3	6	5	0	4	6	3	2	4	1
Libra	1	4	2	3	6	4	0	5	6	3	2	5
Scorpio	4	1	5	2	3	6	5	0	4	6	3	2
Sagittarius	2	5	1	4	2	3	6	4	0	5	6	3
Capricorn	3	2	4	1	5	2	3	6	5	0	4	6
Aquarius	6	3	2	5	1	4	2	3	6	4	0	5
Pisces	4	6	3	2	4	1	5	2	3	6	5	0

KEY

0 = entwined in harmony or locked in death embrace
1 = from different dimensions but understand each other
2 = share elements: siblings under the scales
3 = share energies: alliances of convenience
4 = cannot exist in the same dimension
5 = temporary alliance
6 = long-term alliance

A Grim Glossary

Selected astrological and monster-related terms.

Amulet: a protecting device to guard from evil spirits; can be anything from an incantation to a pentacle, but is often a pendant.

Children of the Night: Dracula's wolf pack border patrol, kept to prevent victims escaping.

Demon: Agent of the Devil. Takes on any size, composition, or shape and can be summoned and controlled by spells and incantation. Metaphorically the spirit that gets into our heads and makes us do bad things.

Ghost: The unquiet spirit of a human being or animal that has lost its physical body. Can manifest anywhere at any time and in any shape or form; been around forever. Metaphorically, our inner fears and self-loathing made almost visible.

Hagstone: A stone with a naturally occurring hole; allegedly made by witches, and worn or hung up on a string to ward off evil.

Moon: Our nearest celestial neighbor; has a physical effect on all the water on Earth, including what's in us. Astrologically, it represents our Inner Selves. Your Inner Self is nuanced by whichever sign the Moon was in at the moment of your birth.

Negative signs: see positive signs.

Pentacle: A pentagram contained in a circle. The five points represent fire, earth, water, air, and spirit. Also known as the Devil's Trap.

Positive and Negative signs: The zodiac has its own binary code that ripples through the signs, alternating between positive and negative. The two groups may also be labeled as masculine/feminine, active/passive, yin/yang, extrovert/introvert. There is no value judgment going on here. It is a description of state: think of it as on/off or odd/even.

Rising Sign: Also known as the Ascendant. The sign coming up on the eastern horizon at the time of your birth. As there are 12 signs and 24 hours in a day, one pops up every two hours, which is why the time of your birth makes a difference to your Rising Sign. Astrologically, Rising Signs represent your outer persona, the face the world sees. I have taken a bit of astro license and interpreted it as how you wish or feel it looks when you are in monster mode.

Ruling Planet: Each sign is associated with a planet (the Sun and Moon count as planets here), and shares the attributes carried by that planet, which are themselves the attributes of the gods the planets are named after. Before the invention of telescopes, stargazers could only see the Sun, the Moon, and five planets Mercury and Venus, Mars, Jupiter, and Saturn. Leo got the Sun, Cancer the Moon, Gemini and Virgo shared Mercury, Taurus and Libra shared Venus, Aries and Scorpio shared Mars, Sagittarius and Pisces shared Jupiter, and Capricorn and Aquarius got Saturn. When Uranus was discovered (1781), it was assigned to Aquarius; in 1846, Pisces got Neptune; and in 1930, Scorpio was given Pluto, although may have to give it back now.

Sun sign: The sign that appears to be behind the Sun (from the Earth's P.O.V.) when you were born. Because it takes us a year to make the orbit, the Sun appears to pass through a sign roughly every month.

Vampire: Undead immortal who needs human blood to survive. Originated in the Carpathian mountains but now spread across the globe; currently enjoying a media moment. Metaphorically, a hypnotically persuasive creature that drains you dry to feed itself.

Werewolf: Human being who regularly transmogrifies into a wolf, usually under the influence of the Moon. Known since the 15th century. Metaphorically the creature that embodies our instinctive unknowable selves, our id.

Index

Acknowledgments

The author (Weremom) would like to thank Jan Johnson (Demon) and
Michael Kerber (Vampire) from Red Wheel Weiser, for taking this on;
her patient and steadfast editor (Vampire) whose heroic resistance to the
temptation of firing a silver bullet in the face of extreme provocation is
exemplary, and the designer and illustrator (Demon) for her talent and the
sprightly wicked images.